The Part That Talks

365 DAYS OF
SCRIPTURAL DEVOTIONS

NORMAN E. WOOD

WRITEWAY PUBLISHING

WRITEWAY
PUBLISHING
www.writewaypublishing.com

DEDICATION

I am pleased to dedicate this work to
Mary Wood,
my wife and my best friend.
She is far more precious than jewels.
(Proverbs 31:10)

PREFACE

My father passed away on a Saturday morning. My daughter, Laurie, was planning to spend part of the day with him before we got the news.

My wife, Mary, and I had decided it was important for Laurie to have closure for her well-loved papa's life, so we scheduled a private viewing at the funeral home the following evening. When we went into the room, Laurie ran across the room to the open casket. She grabbed her papa's fingers, pinched his nose, and commented, "He's really cold."

Mary immediately assumed her role as a good mother and began to try to explain what happens to our souls at death. Laurie, in her own six-year-old fashion, seemed to realize her mother's discomfort in this discussion and replied, "Oh yes, that's the part that talks." Out of the mouths of children come some real spiritual truths…and the title of this book…

The Part That Talks

Rejoice always!
Norm

INTRODUCTION

Regardless of your spiritual or religious orientation, you have a Part That Talks. The Part That Talks is what exhibits your personality, communicates with people verbally, and leaves your body at the time of earthly death. This is your spiritual nature, the part that makes you a person, not the physical parts that are left behind to decay. This book is intended to encourage a special place of meditation where you, the reader, can strengthen and develop your spiritual nature, the part that lives forever, the part that talks. Subject matter will be a selected reading for each day—some scripture, some not—along with a brief commentary that is intended not to preach or offer judgment, but to encourage thought and guide you toward increased awareness of your own spiritual being.

There is no correct or incorrect manner to use these readings. However, for the maximum benefit we suggest that you:

1. Set aside a time each day for reading and meditation, preferably the first thing in the morning ("first fruits of your day") and at the same time each day.
2. Find a private, quiet place to read and meditate, preferably the same place each day.
3. Select the key words, phrases, or thoughts that stand out to you in the reading and keep them in mind throughout the day. You may be surprised at how they impact your day! This can become a topic for meditation and journaling.
4. There are only three "rules" for journaling:
   - Put pen or pencil to paper and write continuously for at least 20 minutes.
   - Do not stop writing—even if you encounter a "writer's block," keep writing.
   - Be totally honest with yourself—you do not have to share the contents.

This is your journey along a spiritual path that will grow more splendid as you grow in knowledge and awareness. Rejoice and enjoy!

Rejoice in the Lord always. I will say it again, Rejoice!
Philippians 4:4

January 1

New Year's Resolutions

... receive instruction in wise dealing, righteousness, justice and equity.
Proverbs 1:3

Many of us begin each new year with resolutions designed to improve ourselves. By the third day, many of us will have already suspended some or all of these resolutions. The Bible gives clear instruction on how to deal with our need for such resolutions: surrender to God's will, commit to living a life of faith, and seek His kingdom first. Everything else will fall into place. Trust in God, and let God do the work.

In order to be the best that we can be, we must surrender completely to God's will. This must be absolute, and it must be complete surrender, not a token acknowledgement.

Peter advised his followers to build their faith with similar commitment in all areas of their lives

...make every effort to supplement your faith with virtue, and virtue with knowledge, and knowledge with self-control, and self-control with steadfastness, and steadfastness with godliness.
2 Peter 1:5-6

Jesus tells us: "...behold, the kingdom of God is in the midst of you" (Luke 17:21). And "...seek first his kingdom and all these things shall be yours as well" (Matthew 6:33).

Carpe diem (seize the day) for a fresh start and surrender to God's will!

REFLECTION

HOW DOES GOD REVEAL HIS PLAN TO YOU?

January 2
No Shortcuts

The Lord is just in all his ways, and kind in all his doings.
The Lord is near to all who call upon him,
to all who call upon him in truth...
Psalm 145:17-18

The place where God ultimately intends for you to be is filled with contentment and prosperity. When you are there, you will be carrying out your part in God's ultimate plan for you. No one else can fill and fulfill this part of God's plan but you.

If you are not yet in this place, you are in the right place to learn and grow. When you fully and faithfully accept being in this place with thanksgiving, you move closer to having the place where you truly want to be and the place where God wants you to be become the same. Therein lies the truth of glorifying God. When we accept with thanksgiving, learn from the experience, and faithfully alter our mentality to be always grateful for His blessings, we glorify God.

Leave simpleness, and live and walk in the way of insight.
Proverbs 9:6

REFLECTION

WHERE IS YOUR "SECRET" PLACE THAT YOU YEARN TO BE?

January 3
The Mental Diet

Do not be not conformed to this world;
but be transformed by the renewing of your mind.
Romans 12:2

Our physical and dietary habits are reflected in our bodies. Likewise, our mental diet is manifested in our mental attitude and our lives.

The things with which we nourish our minds determine the character and condition of our lives. The things we allow our mind to dwell upon, whether negative or positive, are the things that will show and grow in our lives.

You can be transformed. Begin the change with the faithful, daily exercise of loving. Love will heal, comfort, and guide you when you make it the focus of your mental exercises. When negative thoughts enter in, think about love.

We know that in everything God works for good with those
who love him, who are called according to his purpose.
Romans 8:28

REFLECTION

WHAT PEOPLE, PLACES, AND THINGS ARE IN YOUR LIFE
THAT PULL YOU AWAY FROM GOD?

January 4
Divine Guidance

And he said, "My presence will go with you,
and I will give you rest."
Exodus 33:14

In Genesis 33:1, God told Moses to take his followers and go to the land that He had promised. The people had been freed through dramatic divine intervention and Mosaic persuasion. However, Moses' persuasive talents were seriously challenged as he led the people of Israel from Egypt to the Promised Land.

It took 40 years to complete a journey that could have been accomplished in about three weeks if the people had been faithful followers. How often do we take a circuitous route following our own agenda only to find we are not where God meant for us to be? Wait for, listen to, and follow God's will.

Where there is no guidance, a people falls;
but in an abundance of counselors, there is safety.
Proverbs 11:14

REFLECTION

WHO ARE THE LEADERS THAT INSPIRE YOU TO FOLLOW?
WHAT MAKES YOU WANT TO FOLLOW THEM?

January 5
The Yoke

"Come unto me all who labor and are heavy laden, and I will give you rest. Take my yoke upon you, and learn from me; for I am gentle and lowly in heart, and you will find rest for your souls."
Matthew 11:28-29

The yoke is a u-shaped piece that encircles the neck of a draft animal, usually a horse or an ox. The yoke usually is attached to the "burden" of the animal, like a plow or a cart. The animal is strong and able to pull the load comfortably if the yoke is fitted properly. If it is not fitted properly, the yoke can be painful and the burden hard to bear.

Wearing the "yoke" of Jesus means faithfully living in God's will. We can carry the burden, whatever it may be, when we focus on God and trust in Him, knowing that the burden we carry is especially designed for us to carry out our part in His plan.

"Rest for your souls" means rest from the fruitless effort to save ourselves through works but instead accepting gracious respite through God's grace.

"For my yoke is easy, and my burden is light."
Matthew 11:30

REFLECTION

WHAT IS YOUR ATTITUDE TOWARD REST?
DO YOU VIEW REST AS A RESULT OF WEAKNESS OR STRENGTH?

January 6
The Way of Wisdom

Long life is in her right hand; in her left hand are riches and honor. Her ways are ways of pleasantness, and all her paths are peace. She is a tree of life to those who lay hold of her; those who hold her fast are called happy.
Proverbs 3:16-18

There is a story of a king who was miserable and unhappy. He called together all of his magicians, soothsayers, and advisers in hope of finding a solution to his unhappiness. They tried many things, but none worked to bring the king happiness.

Finally, one suggested that they find the happiest man in the kingdom. The theory was that if the king could put on the cloak of the happiest man in the kingdom, he would become happy too. They searched throughout the land and finally found a man who was surely the happiest man in the kingdom. Unfortunately for the king, it turned out that this man had no cloak nor had he ever owned a cloak. His happiness was from within.

Seek to hold the Lord in your heart and build your happiness within. Do not depend on things of this world creating true and lasting happiness for all things of this world are temporary.

You will seek me and find me, when you seek me with all your heart.
Jeremiah 29:13

REFLECTION

HOW WOULD YOUR LIFE CHANGE IF YOU WERE
TO RELY COMPLETELY ON GOD?

January 7
Fear of the Lord

The fear of the Lord is the beginning of wisdom...
Psalm 11:10

Fear of the Lord—meaning reverential awe and admiration—is the foundation of spiritual knowledge. We grow in wisdom, learning what is true, right, and everlasting as our awe and admiration (fear) of the Lord grows through searching for and recognizing His will.

Wisdom yields contentment, longevity, enjoyment, vitality, richness of spirit, and happiness.

Fear of the Lord is the beginning of wisdom. The beginning of our growth is how we share our spiritual knowledge and wisdom with others. Sharing offers unanticipated rewards.

...if you seek it like silver and search for it as hidden treasures;
then you will understand the fear of the Lord
and find the knowledge of God.
Proverbs 2:11

REFLECTION

HOW DOES YOUR REGULAR USE OF TIME, TALENT,
AND TREASURE REFLECT YOUR FAITH?

January 8

Knowing Yourself

...present your bodies as a living sacrifice, holy and acceptable to God,
which is your spiritual worship. Do not be conformed to this world
but be transformed by the renewal of your mind...
Romans 12:1-2

God wants you to be something you have never been. When you hold on to what you are now, or what you once were, you are limiting God's presence and power in your life.

There is a deep-seated passion that dwells in each of us that we may call our "heart's desire." This desire is a key part of our role in God's plan. We accomplish spiritual growth when we identify this desire and clarify it by seeking wisdom and understanding from God. When we apply the wisdom and understanding with no limitations on ways, means, or timing, we open ourselves to what God has in store for us.

"Knowing others is wisdom. Knowing oneself is enlightenment."
Lao Tzu

"Know thyself."
Socrates

REFLECTION

WHAT GIFTS DO YOU HAVE THAT YOU TAKE FOR GRANTED?

January 9
Nothing Is Too Hard

Ah Lord God! It is thou who hast made the heavens
and the earth by thy great power and by thy outstretched arm!
Nothing is too hard for thee...
Jeremiah 32:17

That great, unlimited power that created the universe, made the heavens and the earth, and brought us into the world is always available to us. We find the pathway to perfect solutions when we call upon God without dictating ways or means and trust God to provide His perfect solutions in His perfect timing.

Trust in the Lord with all your heart,
and do not rely on your own insight.
Proverbs 3:5

REFLECTION

HOW CAN YOU TAP INTO GOD'S POWER THIS WEEK?

January 10

Set Sail

The plans of the diligent lead surely to abundance,
but everyone who is hasty comes only to want.
Proverbs 21:5

...the Father who dwells in me does his works.
John 14:10

We have dominion over our own lives. We are captains of our own ships. This is as God intended. However, our ships will never accomplish their missions unless all sails are set. We must pursue our mission with our whole hearts. We begin the journey with "You shall have no other gods before me" (Exodus 20:3). We set the sails after charting the course to work for God's glory.

Go out in peace to love and serve the Lord. When we pursue this journey wholeheartedly, everything falls into place. Ships are safe inside the harbor, but that's not what ships are for.

REFLECTION

WHERE IS YOUR CURRENT JOURNEY TAKING YOU?
WHERE GOD IS SENDING YOU?

January 11

Doubt and Fear

No wisdom, no counsel, no understanding can avail against the Lord.
The horse is made ready for battle, but the victory belongs to the Lord.
Proverbs 21:30-31

We limit God's power in our lives with doubt, fear, and insecurity. When we face problems with prayer, when we expect those prayers to be answered, and when we place total faith in the outcome God can provide, we will come through even our greatest difficulties. In any and all circumstances find contentment in God and nothing else.

Now faith is the assurance of things hoped for,
the conviction of things not seen.
Hebrews 11:1

REFLECTION

WHERE DO YOU NEED TO BE REMINDED OF HIS PRESENCE TODAY?

January 12

The Basics

*Do not be conformed to this world, but be transformed by the
renewing of your mind, so that you may discern what is the good,
pleasing, and perfect will of God.*
Romans 12:2

*Put off your old nature which belongs to your former manner of life
and is corrupt through deceitful lusts, and be renewed in the Spirit of
your minds, and put on the new nature, created after the likeness of
God in true righteousness and holiness.*
Ephesians 4:22-24

Everything else falls into place when we see God and our service to Him as our greatest good. We gain self-confidence by having faith in God's perfect planning and accepting His perfect timing.

Matters of this world cloud the vision. Jobs, social position, and political and work positions of influence are all temporary. There is no lasting satisfaction when our efforts are not in keeping with God's purposes, glorifying Him, and serving His people with sincerity.

REFLECTION

WHAT FALSE SOURCES OF STRENGTH DO YOU RELY ON?
WHY? HOW CAN YOU CHANGE THAT?

January 13

The Lamp

The spirit of man is the lamp of the Lord...
Proverbs 20:27

Do not try to force others to accept spiritual truth. Show them the Light through your own life and conduct. If they are receptive to spiritual truth, the peace and joy that you radiate will attract and motivate them.

"Let your light so shine before men, that they may see your good works and give glory to your Father who is in heaven."
Matthew 5:16

Pray, prepare, have faith, and believe. These are our tasks. Do these tasks and allow God to do His work through you.

REFLECTION

HOW COULD YOU BE MORE INTENTIONAL TODAY IN YOUR
ENCOUNTERS WITH THOSE YOU FIND DISAGREEABLE?

January 14

No Limits

O the depth of the wisdom and knowledge of God!
How unsearchable are his judgments and how inscrutable his ways!
Romans 11:33

God has no limitation. We are the ones who impose limitations. Our minds cannot comprehend the unlimited being of God because of our own limitations. Whatever you think God is, He is that and infinitely more.

When you observe things in nature—flowers, birds, clouds—spend a few moments to consider how they are independent, how they are dependent, and how they make a difference in your world.

From him and through him and to him are all things.
To him be glory forever. Amen.
Romans 11:36

REFLECTION

WHAT ARE THOSE AREAS THAT YOU CONSIDER AS YOUR OWN LIMITATIONS? WHY DO YOU FEEL LIMITED? WHAT WOULD YOU NEED TO DO TO REMOVE OR OVERCOME THOSE LIMITATIONS?

January 15

Give Faith a Chance

"Truly, truly, I say to you, if you ask anything of the Father,
he will give it to you in my name."
John 16:23

Break down old mental concepts of self, limitations, and negativity and build a new concept that has complete faith in God's promises.

Get to work on the most pressing problem you have, probably the one you are most afraid of. Ask God for guidance for resolving the problem. Ask specifically! Pray sincerely. Then consciously, steadily, and faithfully take action. Continue to seek guidance through prayer. Watch and listen for direction to come to you. Keep the positive view you are learning with conscious, steady, and faithful work.

I love those who love me, and those who seek me diligently find me.
Proverbs 8:17 *(Wisdom speaking)*

REFLECTION

WHEN HAVE YOU FELT AT YOUR BEST?
WHEN HAVE YOU FELT AT YOUR WORST?
WHAT WAS THE DIFFERENCE?

January 16

Inner Peace

Agree with God, and be at peace; thereby good will come to you.
Job 22:21

The solution, the only real solution, to all of our problems is to find and consciously know our indwelling Lord. Meditate on this and listen to the divine Power that lives within your soul, seeking it to be present with you in all ways. Pray regularly. Bring your pain and problems before God. Listen to that Power about dealing with those difficulties in your life. Take the most urgent first and the rest in their order of urgency and place them firmly and faithfully in God's hands. As always, seek guidance, have faith, and perform your every act in good will.

Take time to meditate on the results of your prayers. Offer daily blessings back to God in deliberate acts of worship. Give God your praise and your love.

REFLECTION

WHERE DO YOU START?

January 17
The Prince of Peace

... he will make glorious the way...
Isaiah 9:1

*...and the government will be upon his shoulder, and
his name will be called "Wonderful Counselor, Mighty God,
Everlasting Father, Prince of Peace."*
Isaiah 9:6

I saiah is describing the arrival of the Messiah in these passages.

The peace of the Messiah, the peace that passes all under-standing, is where we find our real place in this world. Once true peace of soul is attained, the way is cleared for God to teach us new things, things that are far beyond the scope of this world's under-standing, things that clear the path for even greater peace.

Of the increase of his government and of peace there will be no end...
Isaiah 9:7

REFLECTION

HOW HAS GOD'S CREATION INSPIRED YOU THIS WEEK?

January 18

Build Your House

By wisdom a house is built, and by understanding it is established; by knowledge the rooms are filled with all precious and pleasant riches.
Proverbs 24:2-3

Preparing for our work means prayer, study, and meditation to gain knowledge and understanding of God's will.

Building our house means building our spiritual home as an eternal dwelling place where we are safe, comfortable, and complete with God. We must be an active part of building this relationship with God and actively accept His grace and love.

Prepare your work outside, get everything ready for you in the field; and after that build your house.
Proverbs 24:27

REFLECTION

HOW HAS GOD'S WORK IN YOUR LIFE CHANGED
YOUR OUTLOOK AND YOUR CIRCUMSTANCES?

January 19

Discipline

For the moment, all discipline seems painful rather than pleasant;
later it yields the peaceful fruit of righteousness
to those who have been trained by it.
Hebrews 12:11

Have you ever watched a sporting event in which one team leaves the field or court at the end of the first half seemingly in defeat, only to return with a newly formed game plan and win the game?

This is a good metaphor for our battle against the evil in our lives. With temptation, discouragement, disappointment, and greed, the devil calls us, and we often yield to his call. However, we are forgiven and totally accepted by God in order that we may create a new game plan and regain lost ground.

Read Ephesians 6:11-18. It has a sense of urgency for us to stand firm against the game plan of the enemy. Do not get caught off guard by forgetting that the enemy is constantly in the game of distracting us, disappointing us, misleading us.

If you find yourself going in the wrong direction, regroup and form a new game plan. Remain vigilant and resist the enemy to the death—because that is where he wants to take the struggle. Defeat (spiritual death) is not an option unless we allow it to be.

Put on...compassion, kindness, lowliness, meekness, and patience...
forbearing one another, and...forgiving each other. Above all these put
on love, which binds everything together in perfect harmony.
Colossians 3:12-14

And whatever you do, in word or deed, do everything in the name of

the Lord Jesus, and give thanks to God the Father through him.
Colossians 3:17

REFLECTION

WHAT DISCOURAGEMENT DO YOU FACE TODAY?
HOW WILL YOU HANDLE IT?

January 20
Others

So whatever you wish that men would do to you, do so to them...
Matthew 7:12

We are designed to be here for others. Our purpose on earth is not just for ourselves but to be part of the larger community. We are called to love others. How we relate to others (the kindness and care we show) and how others learn from us are key factors in our own spiritual growth as well as theirs.

"What you do not want done to yourself, do not unto others"
Confucius

"The Way of Heaven is to benefit others and not to injure."
The Way of Lao Tzu

REFLECTION

WHAT WOULD YOU LIKE FOR YOUR FAMILY, FRIENDS,
AND OTHERS CLOSE TO YOU TO REMEMBER ABOUT YOU
AT THE END OF YOUR LIFE ON EARTH?

January 21
Spiritual Discernment

And we impart this [understanding of the gifts bestowed upon us by God] in words not taught by human wisdom but taught by the Spirit, interpreting spiritual truths to those who possess the Spirit.
1 Corinthians 2:13

Spiritual discernment bears little resemblance to human wisdom. Spiritual discernment is the process of intentionally becoming aware of how God is present, active, and calling us as individuals so that we can respond with increasingly greater faithfulness. Spiritual discernment involves seeking God through the means of decision making. Discernment touches on everything to do with our relationship with God. In weighing the decisions, we are looking for signs pointing to God's calling, signs of the present Holy Spirit.

Discernment is a gift.
1 Corinthians 12:4 -10

REFLECTION

TODAY, AS YOU LOOK TO THE DAY AHEAD,
IS YOUR HEART HARDENED? OR IS YOUR HEART CLEAR AND OPEN
TO THE CARES AND CONCERNS OF OTHERS?
WHAT CAN GOD PROVIDE TODAY FOR YOUR HEART?

January 22
Actively Seeking God's Call

The unspiritual man does not receive the gifts of the Spirit of God,
for they are folly to him, and he is not able to understand them
because they are spiritually discerned.
1 Corinthians 2:14

Approaching decision making through spiritual discernment relies on awakening and honing the ability to recognize God's desires in each moment...actively seeking God's call in the very process of making decisions.

We can rely on God to tell us what we need to live properly.
Hebrews 12:2

Discernment is a process—not a product.
I Corinthians 2:14

What no eye has seen, nor ear heard, nor the heart of man conceived,
what God has prepared for those who love him,
God has revealed to us through the Spirit.
1 Corinthians 2:9-10

REFLECTION

HOW HAS GOD FULFILLED YOUR DESIRES RECENTLY?

January 23

For a Happy Life

Rejoice always, pray constantly, give thanks in all circumstances,
for this is the will of God in Jesus Christ for you.
1 Thessalonians 5:16 -18

God is Love. The more we love others, the more we learn about love. The more we know about love, the closer we come to God. The closer we come to God, the more we want to live according to His will and the better we are able to manifest in our lives the things that He wants for us.

Of course, it is good to love and serve others. Generally, they will respond to our treatment by treating us the same way. If they don't, the pleasure of loving and serving is still ours, and the results that come from this may be surprising.

For I know the plans I have for you, says the Lord, plans for good and
not evil, to give you a future and a hope.
Jeremiah 29:11

REFLECTION

HOW HAVE YOU EXPERIENCED THE MAJESTY AND BEAUTY
OF GOD'S PURPOSE AND PLAN RECENTLY?

January 24
Keep the Faith

*Let us not grow weary in well-doing, for in due season
we shall reap, if we do not lose heart.*
Galatians 6:9

We are all here to learn, to learn spiritual lessons that mold us into God's purpose. Even when we are on the mountain top, we are to learn from that experience. Ultimately, we will be given an opportunity to apply what we learned.

When in the valley, we are there to learn lessons that can be learned nowhere else. You can't learn courage from a textbook or a training class. When we ask for courage, God may give us danger to overcome, and we learn. When we seek love, God presents us with opportunities to love others, and we learn.

Face facts, do not try to explain them away. Do not dream about changing the past.

Forget what has happened in the past and focus on what you will make happen in the present.

REFLECTION

WHAT AREAS OF YOUR LIFE OFFER THE MOST OPPORTUNITY
TO LOSE HOPE, FAITH, AND TRUST? HOW CAN YOU PREPARE TO
OVERCOME THESE OBSTACLES?

January 25

The Happy Countenance

Do all things without grumbling or questioning...
Philippians 2:14

We have a choice to be happy—or not to be happy. An unhappy countenance communicates volumes about us and can make others unhappy too. When we grumble or complain, it rarely changes our situation for the better. Often others will respond to our negative feelings in like kind. Unhappiness, bitterness, and suppressed anger are not easily hidden from other people and certainly not hidden from God.

We have a choice to be happy or not to be happy. The genuinely happy person will feel and reflect God's presence and will have a positive impact on every person and every situation they encounter.

...for God is at work in you, both to will and to work,
for his good pleasure.
Philippians 2:13

REFLECTION

WHAT AREAS OF YOUR LIFE SEEM
TO CAUSE YOU TO GRUMBLE OR COMPLAIN?
WHAT CAN YOU DO TO CHANGE YOUR ATTITUDE ABOUT THEM?

January 26

The Tongue

And the tongue is a fire.
James 3:6

What we teach is very important. How we teach is also important. Your tongue can be an instrument of blessing or a painful curse.

Most of us are unaware of just how much we impact others. You never know when you may be the positive—or negative—influence that frames another person's outlook for the day or for a lifetime by the words that come from your mouth.

From the same mouth come blessing and cursing.
James 3:10

REFLECTION

TODAY BE ESPECIALLY AWARE OF THE WORDS YOU SPEAK TO YOURSELF
AND TO OTHERS. SPEAK IN KINDNESS AS OFTEN AS YOU CAN.
DO NOT ALLOW NEGATIVE THOUGHTS TO CONTROL YOUR WORDS.
HOW WILL YOU DEMONSTRATE THIS BEHAVIOR?

January 27

Mistakes

For we all make mistakes…
James 3:2

Over three hundred years ago, Alexander Pope in his "Essay on Criticism" wrote "to err is human, to forgive divine."

When we make mistakes, we can handle them in one of three ways:

- Fix them with whatever corrective action is necessary
- Feature them with self-effacing comments or joking
- Forget them, which is often the best alternative

We need to be quick to forgive mistakes others make. The burden of their mistakes is usually sufficient.

How many blessings or opportunities do we miss as a result of being distracted by mistakes, dwelling on them, and not forgiving ourselves or others for making them?

He who forgives an offense seeks love,
but he who repeats a matter alienates a friend.
Proverbs 17:9

REFLECTION

WHEN, WHERE, AND HOW HAVE YOU SET A BAD EXAMPLE FOR OTHERS?
HOW CAN YOU CHANGE THIS?

January 28

Stir Them Up

...and let us consider how to stir up one another
to love and good works.
Hebrews 10:24

(O)ur purpose for social interaction is not to point out the faults of others but to encourage and be encouraged. When we put out negativity, anger, envy, and anxiety, those emotions are often quickly communicated back to us in turn and have a lasting impact on us and those around us. However, genuine joy, happiness, confidence, and faith are also quickly grasped and felt by those we interact with.

For example, when you walk into a room for a social encounter or a business meeting, you never know how much your attitude will influence another person in the room. Your attitude can change dynamics. Entering with a positive spirit can uplift attitudes. It can reap quietly positive change or dramatic change when you feel and reflect your genuine faith.

Now faith is the assurance of things hoped for,
and the conviction of things not seen.
Hebrews 11:1

REFLECTION

WHAT PLANS HAVE YOU MADE OR WHAT GOALS HAVE YOU SET THAT
GOD INTERRUPTED? WAS THIS A NEW PATH FOR YOU?
DID YOU LISTEN AND FOLLOW?

January 29

Our Competence

...our competence is from God, who has made us competent to be ministers of a new covenant, not in a written code but in the Spirit, for the written code kills, but the Spirit gives life.
2 Corinthians 3:5-6

Jesus discouraged undue emphasis on outer observances and rules. Instead, He emphasized spiritual awareness and observance. When our Spirit is correctly focused, God often takes care of the details.

Commit your work to the Lord, and your plans will be established.
Proverbs 16:3

REFLECTION

WHICH OF YOUR FEARS ARE BASED ON REAL CIRCUMSTANCES?
HOW CAN YOU DIMINISH THAT FEAR?

January 30
Our Skills, God's Results

Do you see a man skillful in his work? He will stand before kings;
he will not stand before obscure men.
Proverbs 22:29

We have all been blessed with certain talents. When we apply these natural talents to daily use, they may develop into true skills through application of time and work.

The gift of talents should not go to waste. If not used, they diminish and ultimately may be lost.

We were given these gifts in order to serve God in a certain way. If we do not respond, God's work will still get done, but we will miss the opportunity to have been part of His work.

REFLECTION

HOW MUST YOU ADJUST YOUR LIFE, HABITS,
AND ATTITUDES TO HEAR GOD'S DIRECTION?

January 31

A Special Place

*And Elijah went up to the top of Carmel; and he bowed himself
down upon the earth, and put his face between his knees.*
1 Kings 18:42

Elijah knew the source of his substantial power, and he consulted the source regularly. Here, he goes to his "special place" at the top of Carmel to be away from worldly distractions so he could be in touch with God.

Having a "special place" is not essential but it can help us get away from the noise and listen. This special place may be nothing more than a special chair where you can sit and focus. Find a place you can call your special place. Go to this place regularly to read a few verses of scripture and reflect on what they are telling you. Open your mind to God's presence and be at peace.

REFLECTION

WHERE DO YOU FEEL CLOSEST TO GOD?

February 1

Search It Out

It is the glory of God to conceal things,
but the glory of kings is to search things out.
Proverbs 25:1

We do not have all the answers, but we can learn the questions. There are many ways we can improve and move more securely toward God's plan. This involves searching on our part. We search things out, seeking truth, truth about our circumstances and about ourselves.

Do you have a trusted friend who can tell you the truth without you being offended? Such relationships are priceless. We cannot respond to what we do not know or see about ourselves. When a trusted friend expresses constructive criticism, it is an act of love. If we are to be the best we can be, we need to know where we fall short so we can take corrective action.

Like a gold ring or an ornament of gold
is a wise reprove to a listening ear.
Proverbs 25: 12

REFLECTION

WHO DO YOU TRUST ENOUGH TO TELL TRUTH TO
AND ACCEPT THEIR CONSTRUCTIVE COMMENTS IN A POSITIVE WAY?
WHY DO YOU TRUST THEM?

February 2

Expectation

*...for I did not receive it from man, nor was I taught it,
but it came through a revelation of Jesus Christ.*
Galatians 1:12

We must not look for God to reveal Himself in any particular way. Often His message comes in the least expected way. What should you do to be ready? Always be in a state of expectancy. Keep your mind and heart centered on right living in accordance with the teachings of Jesus Christ. Do not allow the ways and values of this world to crowd your thoughts and fill your life. Leave room for the Lord.

REFLECTION

TODAY, LOOK FOR NEW OR UNEXPECTED
OPPORTUNITIES TO BE KIND.

February 3
Taking Stock of Ourselves

You have sown much, and harvested little; you eat, but you never
have enough; you drink, but you never have your fill; you clothe
yourselves, but no one is warm.... Consider how you have fared. "...
build the house, that I may take pleasure in it
and that I may appear in my glory...," says the Lord.
Haggai 1:6-8

When the Jews returned to Palestine in 538 BC from captivity in Babylon, they pursued their own interests rather than focusing on rebuilding their Temple so they could worship and honor God. Today's scripture points out that following man's plan instead of God's plan did not work well for them.

To keep from sowing much and harvesting little in our own lives, we need to continually focus on our spiritual lives and be fertile ground for the seeds God wishes to sow through us.

REFLECTION

WHAT ARE THE DISAPPOINTMENTS IN YOUR LIFE THAT
CONTINUE TO OCCUR? HOW WILL YOU HANDLE THEM?

February 4

Change

He changes times and seasons; he removes kings and sets up kings;
he gives wisdom to the wise and knowledge
to those who have understanding...
Daniel 2:21

Unfortunately, all too often people and organizations expect change to come quickly or easily. It does not work that way. Whether we are seeking change inside ourselves or whether we are part of working for change in a larger venue, we need to remain focused on the desired goal in light of God's work. With the right attitude and behavior consistent with our walk with God, with wisdom helped by knowledge, we can work toward affecting the change desired. We must remember this is a process that takes effort, discernment, and continual evaluation of the path.

Jesus Christ is the same yesterday and today and for ever.
Hebrews 13:8

REFLECTION

HOW WILL YOU LEARN TO STOP PRETENDING,
START PERFORMING, AND BECOME MORE REAL
TO YOURSELF AND OTHERS?

February 5

All is Vanity

I have seen everything that is done under the sun; and behold,
all is vanity and a striving after wind.
Ecclesiastes 1:14

There is nothing better for a man than that he should eat and drink,
and find enjoyment in his toil. This, also, I saw,
is from the hand of God.
Ecclesiastes 2:24-25

The first paradigm describes life, despite extreme wealth and material possessions, as vacuous and without reward or meaning. Then God is placed in the center of life and the paradigm changes. Now there is a gracious acceptance of life's pleasures.

Go ahead, enjoy life. Enjoy all of the good pleasures—with God at the center. Allow God, not the pleasure alone, to become the true source of your satisfaction and enjoyment.

O the depth of the riches and wisdom and knowledge of God!
Romans 11:33

REFLECTION

LIST FIVE BLESSINGS IN YOUR LIFE.

February 6
What Is Our Work?

...his occupation is sorrowful...
Ecclesiastes 2:22-23

God designed us for work but work alone does not satisfy. This idea was expressed by Solomon, the richest man in the world. He was wildly successful in the eyes of the world but viewed what he was doing as futile. He expressed that his days were filled with grief and his occupation was sorrowful.

When we make work our purpose, we can never do enough. When we make service our purpose, service first to God and then to others, our work becomes meaningful and rewarding.

Given real peace of soul, all other things fall into place, because we are at a place where we allow Him to teach us new and remarkable things that we otherwise would have missed. When we get a blessing from God, we can give back to Him a love gift by taking time to meditate and offer thanks to Him.

Worship, waiting, and work should always go together.

REFLECTION

WHY DO YOU THINK GOD TRUSTS US TO DO HIS WORK?

February 7
Idol Worship

*"The divine gifts of creation are meant to be enjoyed as matters
of stewardship rather than possession."*
Daniel Treier

Possessions are meant to be received with gratitude and steward-
ed for the benefit of others. Do not make an idol of material
wealth. Net worth does not equal our worth as children of God
in God's image. (See Ecclesiastes 2:10) The law of diminishing returns will set in if we pursue anything out of proportion to its
actual value.

Leave simpleness and live, walk in the way of insight.
Proverbs 9:6

REFLECTION

WHAT ARE YOUR SPECIAL GIFTS?

February 8

Newness of Life

...we also should walk in newness of life...
Romans 6:4

The moment of agreement depends on us—that moment when we bury the old self and walk in the newness of a life with God.

The more we depend on God's help over our major obstacles, the more we realize His constant support during every moment of our journey.

REFLECTION

**HOW DO YOU FEEL ABOUT THE WAY
YOU ARE HANDLING GOD'S BLESSINGS TO YOU?**

February 9
Integrity, Wisdom, and Understanding

He who walks in integrity walks securely...
Proverbs 10:9

Integrity is adherence to a code of values. Other words associated with integrity are uprightness, faith, honesty, and virtuousness. We usually know what the right action is. The challenge is doing it, especially when it seems to be the most difficult choice, but that is integrity.

On the lips of him who has understanding wisdom is found...
Proverbs 10:13

Wisdom is an understanding of what is true, right, or lasting; it is clear thinking and good judgment. Wisdom is the fruit of praying, meditating, studying, and constantly seeking understanding.

Understanding is the path to wisdom, and this path is part of a continuously changing landscape. Wisdom increases as we increase understanding.

REFLECTION

WHAT HAVE YOU UNDERSTOOD TO BE YOUR TRUE CALLING
IN LIFE'S WORK? HOW ARE YOU CARRYING IT OUT?

February 10

Just Do It

Truly, truly, I say to you, if you ask anything of the Father, he will give it to you in my name. Hitherto you have asked nothing in my name; ask and you will receive, that your joy may be full.
John 16:23-24

Identify a concrete problem in your life today. The key is not so much getting rid of your difficulty but rather finding the best way to resolve it. Within every problem are the seeds of a solution. There is also at least one lesson. God wants you to find the solution, learn His lessons from the experience, and apply those lessons to glorify Him. Examine this problem you have identified. Pray about it. Ask God to show you the way and to help you with the lesson you are to learn.

"Ask, and it will be given you; seek, and you will find; knock, and to him who knocks it will be opened."
Matthew 7:7-8

REFLECTION

WHAT IS YOUR SINGLE BIGGEST PROBLEM?
WHERE IS IT WITHIN THAT PROBLEM
THAT YOU SPECIFICALLY WANT GOD'S HELP?

February 11

Preparation

Prepare your work outside, get everything ready in the field,
and after that build your house.
Proverbs 24:27

But seek first his kingdom and his righteousness,
and all these things will be yours as well.
Matthew 6:33

Preparation for any project or endeavor is necessary for successful completion. All too often our preparation includes a list of tasks and no prayerful consideration. We act like "human doings" rather than "human beings." God's work is our endeavor, no matter what the task, and His divine presence is necessary for a just completion and true success.

Prayerfully place God's will first, acknowledging that all things come from Him, and humble yourself to His will.

He who is slack in his work is a brother to him who destroys.
Proverbs 18:9

REFLECTION

WHEN HAVE YOU FELT THE HOLY SPIRIT DIRECTING YOU?

February 12

Walk in the Light

Walk while you have the Light, lest the darkness overtake you;
he who walks in darkness does not know where he goes.
While you have the Light, believe in the Light...
John 12:35

The experience of the Light must be shown rather than told. The experience must be genuine and life altering. Beware of the smug person who has had an experience that he refers back to continuously but who does not work it out in practical daily living—physically, spiritually, and morally.

Walk in the light of the vision that has been given to you. Do not compare yourself to others, do not judge others. They are on their own walk and that walk is between them and God.

...walk as children of the Light (for the fruit of light is found
in all that is good and right and true)...
Ephesians 5:8-9

REFLECTION

HAVE YOU EVER WONDERED IF GOD IS REAL?
WHEN? HOW DID YOU RECONCILE THIS?

February 13

Who Is in Control?

Cast all your anxieties on him, for he cares about you.
1 Peter 5:7

When you put your full faith in God, and by that faith acknowledge that God's will is best for all concerned, life takes on greater dimension, and you are ultimately fulfilled.

What God wants for you is quite possibly far greater than what you want for yourself, only you cannot see it for the clouds of this world that obscure it from your vision.

If you are nervous, intimidated, or afraid, call on God. Know that you are safe in His hands.

If there is someone or something troubling you, look for, and expect to find, the presence of God in that person or that situation.

In all activities affirm your understanding that God (Divine Love) is working for, in, and through you.

We know that in everything God works for good with those who love
him, who are called according to his purpose.
Romans 8:28

All the ways of a man are pure in his own eyes,
but the Lord weighs the spirit.
Proverbs 16:2

For I know the plans I have for you, says the Lord, plans for welfare
and not for evil, to give you a future and a hope.
Jeremiah 29:11

REFLECTION

WHAT KEEPS YOU FROM FEELING JOYFUL?

February 14
Who Is St. Valentine?

There are several conflicting accounts of St. Valentine who inspired the holiday. A favorite is about a man who was martyred in the third century. He was said to have been executed on February 14th probably about 270 A.D. by the emperor Claudius II for helping Christian couples get married. Claudius II thought marriage made his soldiers weak, and therefore, he did not approve of Valentine's work.

As we focus on what this day celebrates for us individually, let's also focus on the true meaning of love in all of its dimensions.

> *Love is patient and kind; love is not jealous or boastful;*
> *it is not arrogant or rude. Love does not insist on its own way;*
> *it is not irritable or resentful; it does not rejoice at wrong but rejoices*
> *in the right. Love bears all things, believes all things, hopes all things,*
> *endures all things. Love never ends...*
> **1 Corinthians 13:4-8**

REFLECTION

WHAT ARE SOME WAYS YOU CAN SHOW YOUR LOVE FOR YOUR SPOUSE? YOUR CHILDREN? YOUR FAMILY AND FRIENDS? OTHER PEOPLE?

February 15
When We Stumble

For we all make many mistakes...
James 3:2

We are totally accepted, just the way we are. There is nothing we can do ourselves to achieve God's grace. We must accept that grace in the same manner it is given—freely, completely, and unconditionally.

Grace is receiving something we don't deserve; mercy is not receiving something we do deserve.

But the wisdom from above is first pure, then peaceable, gentle,
open to reason, full of mercy and good fruits,
without uncertainty or insincerity.
James 3:17-18

REFLECTION

WHEN YOU LOOK AT THE SCARS IN YOUR LIFE,
WHAT DO YOU SEE? WHAT HEALING TOOK PLACE?

February 16
Change

For everything there is a season, and a time for every matter under heaven...
Ecclesiastes 3:1

When a problem or an adverse set of circumstances arises, it often indicates a need for change. Change is constant. How we respond to change reflects the fullness of our understanding.

When we respond to change with fear or anxiety, we lack faith. Granted, change sometimes brings true misfortune and adversity—like loss of health or the loss of a loved one—but most often change is more like upheaval, and we probably need to stop a moment and learn more about what the change is and what it will involve on our part and how it will involve others. We need to look at it from all sides. It may be an opportunity for something new to be experienced. It may be an opportunity for a lesson.

When we respond to change with an open mind and open heart, we can get a good idea of what its impact will be on us and our lives and on those around us. We can appreciate those differences, and we can have a trust in the people involved as well as a trust in God's provision for us.

Faith and trust in God allow us to face change and manage its impact on our lives.

For those who truly trust in God and believe in the power of prayer, change offers a fuller expression of faith.

He has made everything beautiful in its time;
also he has put eternity into man's mind...
Ecclesiastes 3:11

REFLECTION

WHAT EXCUSES DO YOU USE TO PREVENT ANSWERING GOD'S CALL?

February 17

Level Paths and Smooth Sailing

Teach me thy way, O Lord, and lead me on a level path
because of my enemies.
Psalm 27:11

L evel paths to travel are much desired and sometimes hard to
come by. The Romans built many roads. The simple ones were
formed by the dirt thrown from the side of ditches to the center of
a path and then smoothed out, making a road, a level and higher
path open to the public for unrestricted travel.

A level path in life is also much desired and often hard to
come by because of life's ups and downs and by whom or what we
meet on our path.

Often our real enemies on our life's path are our own fears
and doubts. The Psalmist handles these enemies by praying for direction, and then he asks God to lead him on a level path.

When we pray and confront our fears and doubts head on, God
can guide us to the "level path." God intends for us to have control
over our own lives (granting us free will). At the same time, however,
we are to develop wholehearted faith and pursue spiritual growth to
strengthen our relationship with Him and our trust in Him.

...the Father that dwells in me does the works.
John 14:10

REFLECTION

RECALL A TIME OF SUFFERING YOU EXPERIENCED.
WHAT LESSONS DID YOU LEARN THROUGH THAT TIME?

February 18
Without Doubt

*If any of you lacks wisdom, let him ask God, who gives to all men
generously and without reproaching, and it will be given him. But let
him ask in faith, with no doubting, for he who doubts is like a wave
of the sea that is tossed by the wind.*
James 1:5-8

"Doubt is brother-devil to despair."
Friedrich W. Nietzsche

Nothing can spoil a good plan or prayer like doubt, but doubt
is a part of being human. Doubt is real, and we are to deal
with it as we deal with any other force of this world that keeps us
away from God's will. When we face the doubt squarely and overcome it with faith, the faith gets stronger.

You call for faith:
I show you doubt, to prove that faith exists.
The more of doubt, the stronger faith, I say,
If faith overcomes doubt.
Robert Browning ("Bishop Blougram's Apology")

Let all things be done decently and in order.
1 Corinthians 14:40

REFLECTION

WHAT IS A TIME IN YOUR LIFE WHEN ENCOURAGEMENT
WOULD HAVE MADE A REAL DIFFERENCE?

February 19

Think About It

When I think of thy ways, I turn my feet to thy testimonies;
I hasten and do not delay to keep thy commandments.
Psalm 119:59-60

No matter what your problems are, you can determine their importance or impact on your life. You can even find the solutions. You have the power to select and control your thoughts. God wants you to be fruitful and productive, happy and at peace. The best way to achieve this is to realize God's plan for you and follow His will. The way to discern God's will is constant and consistent prayer and meditation (thoughts) on God's presence in your life.

...whatever is true, whatever is honorable, whatever is just,
whatever is pure, whatever is lovely, whatever is gracious,
if there is any excellence, if there is anything worthy of praise,
think about these things.
Philippians 4:8

REFLECTION

HOW CAN YOU PERSIST UNTIL AN ANSWER
TO YOUR PRAYER OR PETITION COMES?

February 20

Confidence in Times of Trouble

To thee, O Lord, I lift up my soul. O my God, in thee I trust,
let me not be put to shame; let not my enemies exult over me.
Yea, let none that wait for thee be put to shame....
Make me to know thy ways, O Lord; teach me thy paths.
Psalm 25:1-2

In Psalm 25, the Psalmist is placing his trust in God's hands. He goes on to describe his current situation and ask for refuge rather than revenge, then he requests direction. He brings his prayer to a rightful conclusion:

May integrity and uprightness preserve me, for I wait for thee.
Psalm 25:21

When God's path is not clearly in view, our own selfish objectives are probably in the way. Prayer and meditation help us put aside our selfish motives. With humble heart and faithful expectation, we can clear the path.

God is faithful. God is always there with us, even when we do not know it.

God is our refuge and strength, a very present help in trouble.
Psalm 46:1

REFLECTION

IF YOU WERE TO TOTALLY LET GO AND LET GOD,
WHAT WOULD THAT LOOK LIKE IN YOUR LIFE TODAY?

February 21
Building Blocks

...those who live according to the Spirit set their minds
on things of the Spirit.
Romans 8:5

...those who plow iniquity and sow trouble reap the same.
Job 4:8

Our thoughts are the building blocks of our lives. If we use negative thoughts, we build negative lives. If we focus on what we lack, we will lack more.

However, if we use positive, loving thoughts to build our lives, the results are positive and loving. When we give of ourselves out of loving appreciation, focus gratefully on what we have, and faithfully anticipate abundance, the result is abundance. When we expect only good, we find the good in all circumstances.

Take delight in the Lord, and he will give you the desires of your heart.
Commit your way to the Lord; trust in him, and he will act.
Psalm 37:4-5

REFLECTION

WHEN HAVE YOU PRETENDED TO BE SOMEONE OR SOMETHING
YOU WERE NOT? WHAT WERE THE RESULTS?

February 22

Stop Limiting God

No wisdom, no counsel, no understanding can avail against the Lord.
Proverbs 21:30

Unfortunately for us, we limit the power of God in our lives due to lack of faith. Our own limitations should not be our focus. When we think our prayers are not being answered, when we lack faith in God's power, we are limiting the power of God to provide His victory in our own "day of battle." We do not know God's plan, but in our faith, we must believe God's plan and His timing are perfect. God will have victory in His own time and will bring His plan to fruition. Our work, our trials, our blessings are all part of the greater glory of God. We are God's children, and we are blessed!

REFLECTION

**WHEN, HOW, AND IN WHAT CIRCUMSTANCES
HAS GOD COME THROUGH FOR YOU TO MEET CHALLENGES?**

February 23
Opportunity and Timing

Observe the right time...
Ecclesiasticus 4:20

Opportunity is everywhere. It really just amounts to our own mental and emotional readiness to see it.

Opportunity was there yesterday. Natural laws do not change. We do the changing by increasing our knowledge and understanding. Airplanes would have been able to fly 2,000 years ago. Telephones could have worked in Roman times. It's not the natural laws that changed from then to today. It's our knowledge and understanding and the application of both.

Likewise, when we work to expand our knowledge and understanding of God's word, we will grow in spirit and be able to do more of God's work as we continue to grow. When we are ready, God will present us with opportunity.

"When the student is ready, the teacher will appear."
Anonymous

REFLECTION

HOW CAN GOD HELP YOU IN YOUR CURRENT CIRCUMSTANCES?

February 24

Busyness

"Martha, Martha, you are anxious and troubled about many things; one thing is needful. Mary has chosen the good portion, which shall not be taken away from her."
Luke 10:41-42

Jesus is telling Martha to be in the moment like her sister Mary. Mary sat at Jesus's feet and listened to His teaching while Martha busied herself. The "one thing" Jesus spoke of is to realize God's presence, and that "the good portion" is His presence with total, complete, and unconditional love for us.

We cannot handle everything on our own, nor is that expected of us by God. When we worry, fear, or doubt, we demonstrate a lack of faith. God wants us to trust Him.

The world is full of opportunities to be distracted, disengaged from God, doubtful. We all are susceptible to these distractions that call us away from the "good portion." However, when we abandon our personal agenda and let God take over, He will work through us toward accomplishing His divine agenda.

REFLECTION

HOW DO YOU RESPOND TO TRIALS, TRIBULATIONS, AND CHALLENGES?

February 25
Listen for the Voice

...the sheep hear his voice, and he calls his own sheep by name and leads them out. When he has brought out all his own, he goes before them, and the sheep follow him, for they know his voice.
John 10:3

Earnestly, tenderly, constantly, God is calling us. We know His voice, and sometimes we follow it. Wherever the path goes, He is leading, though the destination may surprise us. When faced with a decision, a curve in the road, or fork on the path, look for love. Where the most love is, that is where His voice is calling us to go.

"When we love until it hurts, we find not hurt, but more love."
Mother Teresa

Therefore, if anyone is in Christ, he is a new creation; the old has passed away, behold, the new has come.
2 Corinthians 5:17

REFLECTION

WHAT DOES GOD'S VOICE SOUND LIKE TO YOU?

February 26
Our Path to Success

...let us run with perseverance the race
that is set before us, looking to Jesus...
Hebrews 12:1-2

Success, in worldly terms, usually means material, financial, or physical accomplishment. However, joy and satisfaction (real success) come from fulfilling what we are called by God to do. Each of us is called to a purpose, an individual ministry, that is best accomplished by the one called. We hear that call when we submit humbly, willingly, and completely to God's plan. It may come as a small, steady voice or grow from a deep, yearning passion. The work may seem small or insignificant but know that it is not. It is a part of God's plan!

Dispensing with our own agenda and putting aside worldly desires is not an easy task. Once we discover God's call and follow His plan, the world is still there. Material, financial, or physical success may even be part of the plan, but mission accomplishment provides unsurpassed satisfaction.

"It's easy to say 'no' when there is a deeper 'yes' burning within..."
Stephen Covey

"For my yoke is easy, and my burden is light..."
Matthew 11:30

May the Lord direct your hearts to the love of God
and to the steadfastness of Christ.
2 Thessalonians 3:5

REFLECTION

WHAT CONCERNS OR ANXIETIES DO YOU HAVE THAT ARE SENSELESS
WHEN YOU CONSIDER THEM IN THE PERSPECTIVE OF ETERNITY?

February 27
What Do You Really Want?

"What do you want me to do for you?"
Luke 18:41

...The man of God answered, "The Lord is able to give you much more than this."
2 Chronicles 25:9

Nothing is impossible. Some things require supernatural power, but nothing is impossible with God. When we think something we really want is not possible, when we doubt that circumstances can be changed, or when we fear outcomes that never happen, we limit God's influence in our lives to our detriment, but we can never limit God's ability. With God, all things are possible. We can be more fulfilled, more loving and loved, if we know how to ask, truly believe that we can receive, and willingly accept what God wants to give us.

Agree with God, and be at peace; thereby good will come to you.
Job 22:21

REFLECTION

DO YOU THINK IT IS POSSIBLE TO ASK GOD FOR TOO MUCH?

February 28
Cast Your Burden

Cast your burden on the Lord, and he will sustain you…
Psalm 55:22

The verb "cast" means to throw, pitch, or fling—all of which require letting go completely. The psalmist is telling us to throw our burden, whatever it is, on the Lord—to release it completely because He will sustain us.

Why do we find this so difficult? The difficulty of letting go completely is often a result of our lack of faith or our lack of understanding God's power, an automatic response of handling everything our own way. Consider this—the burden may be there to teach us how to let go and trust God to handle it.

"Come unto me, all who labor and are heavy laden,
and I will give you rest.
Take my yoke upon you, and learn from me…"
Matthew 11:28-29

"For my yoke is easy, and my burden is light."
Matthew 11:30

REFLECTION

HOW HAVE YOU BEEN BLESSED TODAY?
HOW WILL YOU BLESS OTHERS IN TURN?

February 29

Things Learned Along the Way

When you lose, don't lose the lesson.
You can only ignore reality for so long.
There is a reason why God gave us two ears and one mouth.

Identify your priorities and stick to them:
- Live where you are happiest
- Make time to do things important to you
- Be with people who fill your heart

Three Rules
- Respect yourself
- Respect others
- Take responsibility for your actions

The best relationship is one in which your regard for each other exceeds your need for each other.

The Five L's of Peace and Happiness:
- Love greatly
- Laugh often
- Listen for God's voice
- Learn from every experience
- Let God do the work

REFLECTION

WHAT ARE THREE LESSONS YOU HAVE LEARNED FROM EXPERIENCE?

March 1

Do It with Your Best Effort

...obey in everything those who are your earthly masters, not with eyeservice, as men-pleasers, but in singleness of heart, fearing the Lord. Whatever your task, work heartily, as serving the Lord and not men...
Colossians 3:22-23

Whatever your task, wherever you are, whoever your earthly service is for...do it as serving God because that's what you are doing whether you know and acknowledge it or not. God has put you where you are for a reason. His reason is to glorify Him. Do everything with gratitude and humility and give it the best you've got. Learn from your job and your life situations. Then glorify God in the process.

Let your light so shine before men, that they may see your good works and give glory to your Father who is in heaven.
Matthew 5:16

REFLECTION

DESCRIBE A TIME IN YOUR LIFE WHEN YOU REALLY FELT ALIVE, IMPORTANT, AND SPECIAL. WHAT MADE YOU FEEL THIS WAY?

March 2

Humility

"Without humility, there is no virtue"
Reverend Father Paul Christy

The fear of the Lord is instruction in wisdom,
and humility goes before honor.
Proverbs 15:33

"Where there is clarity and wisdom, there is neither fear nor
ignorance. Where there is patience and humility,
there is neither anger nor vexation."
Counsels of the Holy Father, St. Francis. Admonition 27

The humility described in the words of Proverbs is defined as deeply respectful. Without humility, all other "virtues" are meaningless descriptions of a person's personality. The truly great person is well aware of where the talents that generate greatness come from and acknowledges these gifts in humble appreciation. Each of us should acknowledge that our talents, whatever they may be, are gifts to be shared.

Before destruction a man's heart is haughty,
but humility goes before honor.
Proverbs 18:12

REFLECTION

WHAT ACT OF HUMILITY HAVE YOU WITNESSED RECENTLY?

March 3

The Life That Wants to Live in You

Happy is the man who finds wisdom,
and the man who gets understanding...
Proverbs 3:13

A student of piano, one who has spent years of practice, discipline, and learning from instruction, has freedom at the keyboard to make and enjoy beautiful music. One who has never had the first lesson, who has never practiced piano, is equally free at the keys, but his efforts produce something quite different.

So it is with spiritual growth. Wisdom and understanding come to those who seek them diligently. They result from personal discipline and consistent efforts of prayer, study, and meditation. Casual efforts result in casual rewards. With consistent time spent on spiritual growth and diligent actions putting the growth into practice, life becomes more fulfilling.

What really matters is not the life you want to live, it's the Life that wants to live in you.

A perverse man will be filled with the fruit of his ways,
and a good man with the fruit of his deeds.
Proverbs 14:14

REFLECTION

WHAT DECISION HAVE YOU MADE THAT WAS DIFFICULT
MORALLY OR SPIRITUALLY? WHAT WERE THE RESULTS?

March 4

Your Gifts

Now, there are varieties of gifts, but the same Spirit; and there are varieties of service, but the same Lord; and there are varieties of working, but it is the same God who inspires them all in every one. To each is given the manifestation of the Spirit for the common good.
1 Corinthians 12:4-7

What is your real passion? When you peel away all the layers of obligation, doubt, and self-deception, what is it that really excites you? *That* is why you are here.

We should honor our obligations and commitments. However, when we let these obligations and commitments supplant our passion, we limit our contribution to the common good and, in the process, we limit our own satisfaction and peace. We limit the blessings God wants to pour into our lives, and the blessings He wants to provide for others through us.

I love those who love me, and those who seek me diligently find me.
Proverbs 8:17

REFLECTION

HOW WILL YOU TRANSITION FROM READING OR HEARING
GOD'S WORD TO LETTING IT TRANSFORM YOUR LIFE?

March 5

Love or Fear—the Choice Is Ours

So we know and believe the love God has for us. God is love, and he
who abides in love abides in God, and God abides in him.
1 John 4:16

All human feelings are based in one of two emotions: love or fear.

We are all blessed with the power of choice. Our lives are reflections of our choices. We can define our future by making good or bad choices.

Anger, doubt, hatred, jealousy, criticism, and envy are all forms of fear. Happiness, joy, feelings of success and accomplishment, appreciation of beautiful things are all forms of love.

Love is creative, fear is destructive. We can choose to live in love.

Love never ends...
1 Corinthians 13:8

REFLECTION

WHAT DO YOU LOVE MOST? IF SOMEONE WERE TO ASK
YOUR FAMILY OR FRIENDS THE SAME QUESTION ABOUT YOU,
HOW WOULD THEY ANSWER?

March 6

The Checkup

...but what we are is known to God,
and I hope it is also known to your conscience.
2 Corinthians 5:11

It is a good idea to take stock of ourselves in the light of God's eyes on a regular basis. Checking our progress on a regular basis—weekly or monthly—is a basic exercise of spiritual goal setting. A spiritual checkup has far greater impact on us and our lives than achieving an earthly goal.

In this process, set goals according to the standards God expects. The Ten Commandments are strong lessons, but the Great Commandment from Jesus—love God and love others—is all-encompassing!

God does not condemn us for falling short; He loves us even when we fall short. Meanwhile, our earthly mission is accomplished with holy intentions when we seek to follow God's will. The results are peace and spiritual growth. The reward for the time spent in spiritual checkups is a greater closeness to our Lord that will far exceed anything material that man can provide.

...do not forget my teaching, but let your heart keep my
commandments; for length of days and years of life
and abundant welfare will they give you.
Proverbs 3:1

REFLECTION

WHY DO YOU THINK IT IS HARD TO GIVE UP
OUR EARTHLY HEROES AND IDOLS?

March 7

Making a Change

But be doers of the word, not hearers only, deceiving yourselves.
James 1:22

For those who seek to become different individuals in the eyes of God and man, the Sermon on the Mount gives definite and specific directions to put into practice.

The word "blessed" comes from a Greek word that can be translated as "happy."

"Blessed are the poor in spirit, for theirs is the kingdom of heaven.
Blessed are those who mourn, for they shall be comforted.
Blessed are the meek, for they shall inherit the earth.
Blessed are those who hunger and thirst for righteousness,
for they shall be satisfied.
Blessed are the merciful, for they shall obtain mercy.
Blessed are the pure in heart, for they shall see God.
Blessed are the peacemakers, for they shall be called sons of God.
Blessed are those who are persecuted for righteousness sake,
for theirs is the kingdom of heaven.
Blessed are you when men revile you and persecute you and utter all
kinds of evil against you falsely on my account. Rejoice and be glad,
for your reward is great in heaven…"
Matthew 5:3-12

Let your light so shine before men, that they may see your good works
and give glory to your Father who is in heaven.
Matthew 5:16

REFLECTION

HOW DO YOU FEEL ABOUT YOUR FUTURE RIGHT NOW, TODAY?

March 8

Blessed Are the Poor in Spirit

"Blessed are the poor in spirit; for theirs is the kingdom of heaven."
Matthew 5:3

Those who let go of personal agendas, release all desire of self-serving, and pursue a wholehearted search for spiritual wellbeing (God's presence) are "the poor in spirit."

This means removing all attachment to material things, personal prejudices, and personal habits in order to clear the channels of connection with God.

Note that this does not mean giving away or throwing away everything you have in order to become "poor." It does mean letting go of prejudices and negativity. It means allowing those material things we enjoy to be recognized as gifts from God and the habits we create in our lives directed as a means to glorify God.

Material things may be utilized to help others in loving fashion. Pursue knowledge to understand your prejudices and along the way attack those prejudices in search of holy meaning and spiritual truth. Replace bad habits with good habits while praising and thanking God for the opportunity to learn more about the good that life has to offer.

God is spirit, and those who worship him
must worship in spirit and in truth.
John 4:24

REFLECTION

WHAT ARE THE CONSEQUENCES YOU EXPERIENCE WHEN YOU WORRY?

March 9

Blessed Are Those Who Mourn

"Blessed are they that mourn: for they shall be comforted."
Matthew 5:4

The emotions we feel and the suffering we experience at the loss of a loved one will ultimately bring us closer to God. Spiritual growth sometimes comes only as a result of such painful experiences.

Do not ignore these emotions, deal with them positively by allowing them to run their course and listen for God's voice in the process.

We gain comfort and end mourning by experiencing the presence of God.

"...I came that they may have life and have it abundantly."
John 10:10

REFLECTION

WHEN IT SEEMS LIKE GOD IS NOT THERE, HOW DO YOU RESPOND?

March 10

Blessed Are the Meek

"Blessed are the meek, for they shall inherit the earth."
Matthew 5:5

Meek is a mental attitude that is often misunderstood as timid, reticent, or weak. However, the real meaning is quite different in the Bible. There, meek expresses confidence, strong faith in God, and willingness to do right and follow God's will without concern for the attitudes of the world.

The earth, in this discourse, is essentially the whole of our outer experience, the universe around us. To inherit is to receive possession or control over something. Thus, "inherit the earth" means to receive dominion over our outer experience—our environment—as a result of having confidence, a strong faith in God, and a willingness to follow God's will.

"...the Father, who dwells in me does his works."
John 14:10

REFLECTION

WHAT EVIDENCE DO YOU SEE THAT GOD
HAS YOUR BEST INTERESTS IN MIND?

March 11

Blessed Are Those Who Hunger

*"Blessed are those who hunger and thirst for righteousness,
for they shall be satisfied."*
Matthew 5:6

Self-control, self-discipline, prayer, meditation, and sincere effort to do the right thing for the right reason(s) will ultimately lead to satisfaction. Even as we fall short of righteous perfection, the journey yields a degree of satisfaction that could not have been realized otherwise.

Those who genuinely seek righteousness discipline themselves inwardly as well as outwardly. These behaviors also have a positive influence on other people. The reward for these behaviors is the satisfaction of greater closeness to God and awareness of God's appreciation of our efforts.

Growing closer to God takes deliberate pursuit and attentiveness.

*To do righteousness and justice is more acceptable
to the Lord than sacrifice.*
Proverbs 21:3

He who pursues righteousness and kindness will find life and honor.
Proverbs 21: 21

REFLECTION

LIST THREE THINGS YOU COULD DO TO IMPROVE YOUR PHYSICAL
HEALTH AND THREE THINGS TO IMPROVE YOUR SPIRITUAL HEALTH.

March 12

Blessed Are the Merciful

"Blessed are the merciful, for they shall obtain mercy."
Matthew 5:7

This theme about our mental state and our thoughts toward others is repeated throughout the Sermon on the Mount and beyond:

"...everyone who is angry with his brother
shall be liable to judgment..."
Matthew 5:22

"...love your enemies and pray for those who persecute you."
Matthew 5:44

"Judge not that you be not judged."
Matthew 7:1

"For with the judgment you pronounce you will be judged
and the measure you give will be the measure you get."
Matthew 7:2

You, yourself, will ultimately receive the same treatment you apply to others. You will receive the same merciful help in your time of need that you give others.

We have no right, no authority, no reason to judge or condemn others.

We are placed here to help others, not to judge them.

REFLECTION

HOW DO YOU SHOW LOVE TO SOMEONE YOU DO NOT KNOW WELL
BUT WHO NEEDS TO KNOW GOD'S LOVE?

March 13

Blessed Are the Pure in Heart

"Blessed are the pure in heart, for they shall see God."
Matthew 5:8

When we "see" God, we experience Heaven as it really is. Our spiritual perception means our capacity to experience God's presence where we are. The heavenly requirement is that we remove anger, jealousy, lust, envy, greed, pride, and all negativity in order to become "pure in heart."

Achieving such a state offers us total freedom, happiness, and the awareness of Truth.

REFLECTION

DO YOU HAVE A FRIEND OR RELATIVE WHO IS YOUR
"ACCOUNTABILITY PARTNER?" DO YOU THINK HAVING AN
ACCOUNTABILITY PARTNER IS IMPORTANT?

March 14

Blessed Are the Peacemakers

"Blessed are the peacemakers; for they shall be called sons of God."
Matthew 5:9

This refers not only to peaceable persons, but also to those who work to make peaceful resolutions and spread peaceful experience in their everyday endeavors.

Those who wish to become peacemakers will find that the most effective path to genuine change of character is prayer and consistent communion with God. This sense of the presence of God offers confidence and true peace of mind.

REFLECTION

WHAT ARE SOME COMMENTS OR QUESTIONS YOU COULD USE
TO START A CONVERSATION ABOUT YOUR FAITH
AND THE PEACE IT BRINGS?

March 15

Blessed Are Those Who Are Persecuted

"Blessed are those who are persecuted for righteousness' sake, for theirs is the kingdom of heaven. Blessed are you when men revile you and persecute you and utter all kinds of evil against you falsely on my account. Rejoice and be glad, for your reward is great in heaven..."
Matthew 5:10-12

This does not say that you must be persecuted in order to be blessed. It does say that when you are persecuted for righteousness' sake, you will find a reward—the kingdom of heaven. We gain the kingdom of heaven by cultivating serenity or peace of mind and soul. This will generate jealousy among those who have no such serenity. Their response may be resentment, jealousy, even persecution. This Beatitude is telling us to pay no attention to that jealous manifestation but to continue in serenity, knowing that any physical suffering can be transcended by our spiritual response.

God asks us to accept His rewards of peace, prosperity, and salvation. We must accept His gifts and allow Him to put things right. If we respond to persecution with acts or even thoughts of vengeance, we limit what God wants to give us. Persecution may become a blessed condition when we remember that everything God places in our path contains a lesson which, properly learned, will lead to spiritual advancement and increased peace.

"Be faithful unto death, and I will give you the crown of life."
Revelation 2:10

"Rejoice and be glad, for your reward is great in heaven..."
Matthew 5:12

REFLECTION

WHAT AREAS OF YOUR LIFE ARE CALLING YOU
TO TAKE A FIRM STAND FOR YOUR FAITH?

March 16

A New Commandment

"A new commandment I give to you, that you love one another;
even as I have loved you, that you also love one another."
John 13:34

Let love be genuine; hate what is evil, hold fast what is good; love one
another with brotherly affection; outdo one another in showing honor.
Never flag in zeal, be aglow with the Spirit, serve the Lord. Rejoice in
your hope, be patient in tribulation, be constant in prayer.
Romans 12:9-12

You are a sacred product of God's creation. You are precious in God's eyes. You were made to be loved, honored, and respected. And so it is with all of God's creation and God's people.

No one has the divine authority to diminish or demean you. When we allow the words or actions of others to compromise our sacred purpose, we are compromising God's purpose.

Love does no wrong to a neighbor;
therefore, love is the fulfilling of the law.
Romans 13:10

REFLECTION

DESCRIBE A TIME WHEN SOMEONE MADE A SACRIFICE FOR YOU.
HOW DID YOU RESPOND?

March 17

Do It from Love

A cheerful heart is a good medicine...
Proverbs 17:22

Do things out of sheer love of God. To serve God is a deliberate act, a love-gift expressing His nature in us. We serve Him in the ordinary ways of life out of devotion to Him.

There is a lesson to learn in every condition we encounter in our lives. When we face those situations from a perspective of love, our perspective is positive and encouraging to ourselves and other people.

A glad heart makes a cheerful countenance,
but by sorrow of heart the spirit is broken.
Proverbs 15:13

REFLECTION

HOW WOULD YOU DESCRIBE BEING FILLED BY THE SPIRIT?

March 18
The Shepherd

The Lord is my shepherd, I shall not want;
he makes me lie down in green pastures...
Psalm 23:1-2

The shepherd starts early leading his sheep to pastures. The sheep walk steadily. They are never still as they graze. By late morning, the sheep are hot, tired, and thirsty. The shepherd knows that they must not drink when their stomachs are filled with undigested grass, especially when it is hot. The wise shepherd makes the sheep lie down. They will not eat lying down, so they chew their cud, which is nature's way of digesting their food.

When we are like the sheep, accepting our Shepherd's commands as being for our best interest, He is protecting us from the consequences that result from following our own devices.

We make considerable effort to succeed in the world's view. Hard work, strategic planning, skillful efforts, all to accomplish what we think is in our best interests. None of these is bad when properly applied. They are methods that allow us to accomplish things. However, the path to real success is the path that God puts us on when we open our minds and hearts to His will.

We find and focus on this path when we stop, pray, and listen.

"Be still, and know that I am God."
Psalm 46:10

REFLECTION

**WHY DO YOU THINK IT IS IMPORTANT TO FOLLOW
GOD'S WILL IN YOUR ACTIONS?**

March 19

Judging Others

Do not judge by appearances, but judge with right judgment.
John 7:24

Jesus sees us as we really are, not as we appear to others. He sees our spiritual self. This spiritual self is divine and perfect. Those around us cannot see it. Those with clear understanding and wisdom can see portions of it, but only our Lord sees the whole spiritual self.

Everyone has a divine, spiritual self. When we seek the presence of Christ in others, their outer appearance may become different, and our attitude toward them takes on a new perspective.

When we consistently seek to see Christ in others, we find Him in ourselves. Likewise, the more readily then is Christ seen in us by others.

For now we see in a mirror dimly, but then face to face.
Now I know in part; then I shall understand fully,
even as I have been fully understood.
1 Corinthians 13:12

REFLECTION

WHAT HAVE YOU LEARNED FROM THOSE WHO
DISAGREE WITH YOU OR PERSECUTE YOU?

March 20

The Caterpillar

... no eye has seen, nor ear heard, nor the heart of man conceived,
what God has prepared for those who love him...
1 Corinthians 2:9

Can you think of anything more limited in its existence than a caterpillar? The caterpillar moves very slowly over a small space during its entire life as a caterpillar. Then things change. It faithfully spins its cocoon and goes to sleep, allowing nature to take its course.

This process provides the growth necessary for it to have wings, to fly unrestricted, and become what God planned for it.

For everything there is a season,
and a time for every matter under heaven.
Ecclesiastes 3:1

REFLECTION

HOW HAS HEALING FOR YOU OR A LOVED ONE
OCCURRED IN WAYS YOU NEVER EXPECTED?

VERNAL EQUINOX

A Time to Plant

*For everything there is a season, and a time for every matter under
heaven... a time to plant...*
Ecclesiastes 3:1

The vernal equinox, which falls about March 20 or 21 in the Northern Hemisphere, is a time when the sun crosses the celestial equator and day and night are of equal length.

Nature makes this an optimum time to plant. The spring thaw follows the winter freeze, and the melting snow was full of nutrients that now inhabit the soil. The dairy animals consume the resulting flowering plants and grasses. In many cases the milk and cheese products are considered the best of the year in terms of flavor.

Now is the time to plant, or re-plant, seeds that will generate your goals.

REFLECTION

WHAT SEEDS HAVE YOU PLANTED?

March 21

The Butterfly

For it is precept upon precept, precept upon precept,
line upon line, line upon line...
Isaiah 28:10

A young boy found a cocoon on a leaf. He noticed that it was partially torn. Upon closer inspection, he discovered that the tear was a result of the caterpillar inside struggling to exit. In excited sympathy, the boy took his knife and helped the caterpillar by cutting the opening in the cocoon, allowing the caterpillar to break free.

The caterpillar emerged from the cocoon as a beautiful butterfly. It spread its beautiful wings, jumped off the leaf, and fluttered to the ground where it died. The young boy did not realize that the struggle he witnessed was God's way of building strength in the butterfly's wings, so it could fly.

Whether we face triumphs or disasters, we are here to grow, to learn something that prepares us for the next phase of God's plan for our lives. Self-pity accomplishes nothing. Self-examination and determination will help us focus. Faith and trust in God will allow us to experience this growth in the manner that God is providing, in order that our accomplishments may glorify Him.

REFLECTION

WHAT TRIALS DO YOU FACE THAT CONTAIN
LESSONS FROM PAST TRIALS?

March 22

Be Bold

And now, Lord, look upon their threats, and grant to Thy servants to speak Thy word with all boldness...

Acts 4:29

Boldness is not a brash, foolhardy mentality. Boldness implies deliberate action from a deliberate decision, although sometimes it seems like "biting off more than you can chew."

Be bold and mighty forces will come to your aid.

The "mighty forces" referred to are the forces of your skill, energy, good judgment, and your creative ideas that will propel you to accomplishing the goals you set.

REFLECTION

WHAT ARE YOUR THREE GREATEST FEARS THAT KEEP YOU FROM BEING BOLD?

March 23

Stand Firm

Be watchful, stand firm in your faith; be courageous, be strong.
1 Corinthians 16:13

The directions are clear. Being watchful requires knowing what to watch for—false prophecy, false teaching, and the like. Being strong, being courageous, and standing firm in our faith all require preparation, training, and spiritual growth. Strength is built through consistent exercise; courage comes from experience and trust.

It is very easy to adopt the ways of the world. Peer pressure and inertia are powerful forces. It is also easy to rationalize behaviors that we know are not right.

The right spiritual path is not an easy one. We engage with the world—in our work, our relationships, and our daily activities—because we are human. However, we really are spirits in a human existence, and the spiritual work is the most significant. Faith, prayer, meditation, and studying God's word all help us find and remain on the spiritual path.

Let all that you do be done in love.
1 Corinthians 16:14

REFLECTION

HOW DO YOU FEEL BLESSED TODAY?

March 24

Paradox

"A new commandment I give to you, that you love one another;
even as I have loved you, that you also love one another."
John 14:32

The word paradox comes from the Greek word *paradoxos,* which means conflicting with expectation. Webster defines paradox as a seemingly contradictory statement that may nonetheless be true.

Restating the Webster definition paradoxically, we come up with "truth may seem to be a contradictory statement."

We find truth when we observe the paradox in celestial terms like love, hope, giving—as in "more blessed to give than to receive."

It is in loving others that we feel the greatest rewards of love. The more we love other people, the more we see other people to love, and the more we feel the love of God for us.

I love those who love me, and those who seek me diligently find me.
Proverbs 8:17

REFLECTION

WHERE DO YOU SEE AN EXAMPLE THAT
TRUTH MAY SEEM TO BE A CONTRADICTORY STATEMENT?

March 25

Be at Peace Among Yourselves

Be at peace among yourselves.
1 Thessalonians 5:13

When we have our own agenda (God has a plan, but I have a better idea…) and implement it with selfish pride, we always come up short. We often end up having to pray for God to help us out of a mess.

When we have genuine peace with ourselves, with God, and with others, we accomplish great things—things God wants us to accomplish. The results and the rewards far exceed anything we could desire or hope for.

And we exhort you, brethren, admonish the idlers, encourage the fainthearted, help the weak, be patient with them all.
1 Thessalonians 5:14

REFLECTION

WHAT EXAMPLES OF A SPIRITUALLY BROKEN WORLD
DO YOU SEE TODAY? HOW CAN YOU HELP CHANGE IT?

March 26

Take Up Your Cross

And he said to all, "If any man would come after me, let him deny himself and take up his cross daily and follow me."
Luke 9:23

The cross was a Roman method of execution. In this process, the condemned person carried the cross to the point of execution. Here Jesus is telling His disciples that to follow Him meant pain and anguish, even condemnation, in this world. He did not come to make peace, He came to give peace to those who followed Him in faith, accepting the threat of destruction in this world.

...make every effort to supplement your faith with virtue, and virtue with knowledge, and knowledge with self-control, and self-control with steadfastness, and steadfastness with godliness, and godliness with brotherly affection, and brotherly affection with love. For if these things are yours and abound, they keep you from being ineffective or unfruitful in the knowledge of our Lord Jesus Christ.
2 Peter 1:3-7

REFLECTION

WHAT ARE YOU SACRIFICING FOR THOSE EARTHLY THINGS THAT MATTER MOST TO YOU? WHAT ARE YOU SACRIFICING FOR GOD'S PURPOSE IN YOUR LIFE?

March 27

Faith, Hope, and Love

So faith, hope, love abide, these three; but the greatest of these is love.
1 Corinthians 13:13

God is love, and God's love for us is a special gift. 1 Corinthians 13 contains a beautiful and complete definition:

Love is patient and kind; love is not jealous or boastful; it is not arrogant or rude. Love does not insist on its own way; it is not irritable or resentful; it does not rejoice at wrong but rejoices in the right. Love bears all things, believes all things, hopes all things, endures all things.
1 Corinthians 13:4-7

These verses do not say that "the greatest of these is *being* loved" nor do they indicate control or possession of another person. God loves us, all of us, totally, completely, and unconditionally. This is how we are to love others, all others. When we truly love another, the real reward, the real pleasure in that relationship is in loving that person totally, completely, and unconditionally.

God already loves us totally, completely, and unconditionally, just as we are. The joy of God's love grows as we feel and show that love to and for others in the same manner.

Love never ends.
1 Corinthians 13:8a

REFLECTION

WHO IS YOUR CLOSEST FRIEND? WHY?

March 28

Abide in Him

... abide in him...
1 John 2:28

*"Certainty is the mark of the common-sense life:
gracious uncertainty is the mark of the spiritual life."*
Oswald Chambers

"Gracious uncertainty" or spontaneity is the mark of a spiritual
life. We do not know for certain what comes next, but when
it comes, we greet it with cheerful expectation. The only certainty
is the presence of God.

*But the path of the righteous is like the light of dawn,
which shines bright.*
Proverbs 4:18

REFLECTION

WHAT GOOD WORKS ARE YOU BEING LED TO DO?

March 29

Walk by Faith

...for we walk by faith, not by sight.
2 Corinthians 5:7

Even in the most difficult of times, God is creating something beautiful. There is always hope, and there is always God's plan that may be revealed to us through the perspective that difficulties provide. How can we learn courage if we never face danger?

We are here as men and women in the world to do God's work. When we are grounded in faith, God provides us with infinite power to endure the turmoil, confusion, and chaos.

Therefore do not throw away your confidence, which has a great reward. For you have need of endurance, so that you may do the will of God and receive what is promised.
Hebrews 10:35-36

REFLECTION

HOW CAN YOU BE MORE INTENTIONAL ABOUT YOUR FAITH
IN YOUR DAILY ROUTINE?

March 30

Appearances

For everything there is a season,
and a time for every matter under heaven...
Ecclesiastes 3:1

There are certainly times when we are perplexed by what seems like inconsistencies of life. This is because we only get a partial view of the whole picture. If we could see the whole picture, we would see that what we think of as inconsistencies, or even accidents, are really part of an orderly pattern that culminates in the accomplishment of God's plan.

When we achieve more understanding, we see God's expressions in what we think of as new ways. These are not new ways at all. These are not improvements of God's plan. They have been there all along. What has changed is our understanding and our perspective on God's perfect plan and God's wonderful universe.

REFLECTION

WHAT EARTHLY THINGS MATTER MOST TO YOU? WHY?

March 31

Never Look Back

Another said, "I will follow you, Lord, but let me first say farewell to those at my home." Jesus said to him, "No one who puts his hand to the plow and looks back is fit for the kingdom of God"
Luke 9:61-62

Anyone who has ever plowed a field, whether in a modern tractor or behind a plow horse, knows that if you look back while plowing, your path will not be straight, and the entire field will reflect that. Keeping your eyes fixed on a distant point in front of you will enable you to plow a straight path.

When God puts us on His path, the same principles apply. If we are to plow a straight path toward the life God has for us, we must leave the past where it is, move ever forward, and keep our eyes on the goal.

...let him who is in the field not look back. Remember Lot's wife.
Luke 17:31-32

REFLECTION

JESUS OFTEN USED AGRARIAN METAPHORS TO ILLUSTRATE TRUTH. WHY DO YOU THINK HE DID THIS?

April 1

Claim It and Believe It

"Ask, and it will be given you; seek, and you will find; knock, and the door will be opened to you. For everyone who asks receives, and he who seeks finds, and to him who knocks it will be opened."
Matthew 7:7-8

We open the door for God to pour blessings into our lives when we

- make our claim for God's inspiration, and believe it.
- express belief in His healing, and believe it.
- thank God in advance for peace, harmony, and spiritual growth, and believe it.

We must clear our channels and allow for these things to come to us in abundance. We can achieve this when we

- forgive others without exception and mean it.
- ask God to forgive us for all the sins and errors we have ever committed, fully accept His forgiveness, and mean it.

Think about God, remembering all that you know to be true about Him: His goodness, His perfect timing, His unlimited power, His boundless love, His divine intelligence, and any other characteristics you know. Fully believe in God's wondrous attributes. Believe that God loves you and has a plan for you.

REFLECTION

PAUL TELLS US IN EPHESIANS 2:10 THAT WE ARE CREATED FOR
GOOD WORKS. WHAT DO YOU THINK HE MEANT?

April 2
Deliberate, Purposeful Action

Finally, brethren, rejoice. Become mature, be encouraged,
be of the same mind, be at peace,
and the God of love and peace will be with you.
2 Corinthians 13:11

When we are studying a scripture passage, it can be helpful to understand the fuller meaning of certain words used in their original language. In this passage "become mature" is the translation of the Greek word *katartizo*. This same word also can be translated as "aim for perfection" or "aim for restoration." It can be understood as meaning to mend, to equip, or to make ourselves what we ought to be. All of these are active verbs. They express deliberate, purposeful action rather than passive acceptance.

Becoming mature in true faith is active, purposeful, and deliberate. Faith requires work on our part, and sometimes hard work, but the work leads to our maturity in faith and makes us able to be who and what we ought to be.

Now may the God of peace who brought again from the dead our
Lord Jesus, the great shepherd of the sheep, by the blood of the eternal
covenant, equip you with everything good that you may do his will,
working in you that which is pleasing in his sight,
to whom be glory forever and ever. Amen.
Hebrews 13:20-21

REFLECTION

WHAT DELIBERATE, PURPOSEFUL ACTIONS DO YOU FIND
MOST PRODUCTIVE IN YOUR DAILY WALK WITH GOD?

April 3

Listen and Learn

*Listen to advice and accept instruction, that you may gain wisdom
for the future. ...it is the purpose of the Lord that will be established.*
Proverbs 19:20-21

It is God doing the work. We are the channel through which His
acts are demonstrated. Our duty is to get out of our own way
and allow His plan to unfold.

When God gives a vision and darkness follows, wait. His
silence is a time of discipline, not displeasure. Know that God is
real, and His plan is unfolding.

*...Jesus looked at them and said to them, "With men this is impossible,
but with God all things are possible."*
Matthew 19:26

REFLECTION

WHAT DO YOU FOCUS ON MOST DURING YOUR QUIET TIMES?

April 4

What Is Failure?

...for a righteous man falls seven times and rises again;
but the wicked are overthrown by calamity.
Proverbs 24:16

When we fail, we are given an opportunity to learn and grow. Failure is nothing more than a result. Whatever the failure, it is never final. This applies in daily living and in spiritual growth.

However, since failure is just a result, we can look at the result and learn what to modify in order to change that result. Many of today's successes began as failures that were modified by those who committed them. Failure is merely a growth opportunity.

"Our greatest fear should not be of failure but of succeeding
at things in life that don't really matter."
Francis Chan

He who pursues righteousness and kindness will find life and honor.
Proverbs 21:21

REFLECTION

WHAT FAILURE IS MOST FRIGHTENING TO YOU? WHY?

April 5

Outlining

...continue in the fear of the Lord all day. Surely there is a future,
and your hope will not be cut off.
Proverbs 23:17-18

We are meant to be reflections of God's glory. Others will see this reflection and respond. Their response is not for us to determine. Our responsibility is to learn how to keep seeing God in all circumstances, knowing that He is working through us and through others as they see that reflection.

We are often guilty of "outlining" the result we anticipate. Outlining means drawing or defining the shape of the result we expect. Do not outline. This only delays the demonstration God has prepared. Leave the ways and means to God. Be quiet, be patient, believe and focus on God.

And we all...beholding the glory of the Lord,
are being changed into his likeness...
2 Corinthians 3:18

REFLECTION

WHAT AREAS OF YOUR LIFE REQUIRE EXTRA ATTENTION
TO KEEP FROM STRUGGLING WITH GOD?

April 6

Forgiveness

"And forgive us our debts, as we also have forgiven our debtors…"
Matthew 6:12

Forgiveness is God's plan, not just a part of His plan, but it is God's whole plan. When we accept the fact that we are totally accepted, totally forgiven, we are able to pursue a productive life with God at the center.

When we dwell on doubt, fear, or any other anxiety of this world, we are being selfish and self-centered, and we are not able to accomplish our purpose effectively.

When we dwell on guilt, we are focused on past events that cannot be changed. Don't dream about changing the past. Don't worry about what has happened. Instead, focus on what you are going to make happen in a deliberate, positive way.

REFLECTION

HOW DO YOU DEAL WITH FORGIVING OTHERS?
HOW DO YOU KNOW WHEN YOU HAVE BEEN FORGIVEN?

April 7

We Don't Always Know
What We Sow

…one sows and another reaps.
John 4:37

In this passage, Jesus is telling His disciples that sowing and reaping in the kingdom are ultimately linked, though not immediately.

We may never see the results of what we sow, but sow we do. Your behavior today may influence another's outlook on the world for the rest of his or her life. When we encounter disappointment or trouble, others are often watching. Likewise, when we experience victories, others are often watching. What we do "in the moment" certainly has results in our own lives, and it often impacts lives where we least expect it or may never know.

REFLECTION

DESCRIBE A TIME WHEN SOMEONE YOU TRUSTED PUT YOUR NEEDS AHEAD OF THEIRS. HOW DID YOU FEEL? HOW DID YOU RESPOND?

April 8

Real, Lasting Leadership

It is he...who brings princes to nought,
and makes rulers of the earth as nothing.
Isaiah 40:22-23

The forces of power, greed, and lust have led many people into roles of leadership. Some even conquered "the world" as it was known to them.

"Rulers of the earth" brings to mind rulers like Alexander the Great, who had conquered all of Eastern Europe, Egypt, Asia Minor, the Middle East, Persia, Mesopotamia, and Syria, by the age of 30. Julius Caesar became the namesake for "ruler" all the way to Czars and Kaisers.

The list goes on: Genghis Khan, Hitler, Stalin, and Hirohito. All "rulers of the earth" who conquered by killing others.

Jesus killed no one, fought no one. He never traveled far from home, left no financial fortune. He had no throne, no golden crown. He taught, healed, and loved those who would allow it. Yet, Jesus, who did not begin His ministry until He was 30 and died three years later as a result of execution, brought us a Kingdom which has no end.

"Leadership is not about titles, positions, or flow charts.
It is about one life influencing another."
John Maxwell

REFLECTION

WHICH STORY OF JESUS PROVIDES THE MOST INSPIRATION TO YOU?

April 9

The Spiritual Path

Happy is the man who finds wisdom,
and the man who gets understanding.
Wisdom, understanding, and peace are characteristics
of one who has achieved spiritual fulfillment.
Proverbs 3:13

The cosmic battle to keep you from achieving spiritual fulfillment is constant and consistent. On the path to spiritual fulfillment, we encounter temptations. Most temptations fall under one of five categories:

1. Greed
2. Control over others
3. Mistaken loyalty

4. Bodily temptations
5. Vanity

We all encounter temptations. The readings for the next five days will suggest strategies for handling them.

But as for you, man of God, shun all this; aim at righteousness,
godliness, faith, love, steadfastness, gentleness.
Fight the good fight of faith.
1 Timothy 6:11-12

REFLECTION

MAKE A LIST OF THE TEMPTATIONS THAT MOST OFTEN CALL TO YOU.
HOW DO YOU RESPOND TO THEM?

April 10

Greed and Love of Money

But those who desire to be rich fall into temptation,
into a snare, into many senseless and hurtful desires
that plunge men into ruin and destruction.
1 Timothy 6:9

Greed can assume many personalities. Greed for money and material objects is self-evident. Worshiping these things leads to shallow existence and misery. You can never obtain enough. There is always something more to want.

Greed can also consume us with the desire to be considered important.

Greed can be for the power and position this world offers to those who have material wealth.

It is not money, but the love of money, the desire to be rich, that plunges people into ruin and destruction when they are victims of its temptation.

Instead of seeking wealth and material things, seek to shift your perspective to appreciate each thing that comes into your life for its true value. You will find it's not the material things that bring the most satisfaction.

For the love of money is the root of all evils; it is through this craving
that some have wandered away from the faith
and pierced their hearts with many pangs.
1 Timothy 6:10

REFLECTION

ASSESS HOW YOU GAIN AND SPEND YOUR RESOURCES.
WHAT AREAS NEED GOD'S ATTENTION?

April 11

Power and Control Over Others

The desire for personal power over other people—to make them see it our way or use them to our own benefit—is another temptation that diverts us from the spiritual path.

Religious tyranny is poisonous to its victims and disrupts their spiritual journey. However, it is ultimately far more destructive to the tyrant than the victim as it separates the tyrant from God.

Lord, make us instruments of your peace. Where there is hatred, let us sow love; where there is injury, pardon; where there is discord, union; where there is doubt, faith; where there is despair, hope; where there is darkness, light; where there is sadness, joy. Grant that we may not so much seek to be consoled as to console; to be understood as to understand; to be loved as to love. For it is in giving that we receive; it is in pardoning that we are pardoned; and it is in dying that we are born to eternal life. Amen
A prayer attributed to St. Francis

REFLECTION

HOW DOES AN ETERNAL PERSPECTIVE
CHANGE YOUR ACTIONS AND CHOICES TODAY?

April 12

Mistaken Loyalty

"I am the way, and the truth, and the life;
no one comes to the Father, but by me."
John 14:6

We are on a personal journey as one of God's children. We search for the Way, the Truth, and the Life—Christ. Our individual progress along the path can be diverted by mistaken loyalty to people or places whose sole purpose should be showing us the way to that end. Churches, ministries, or religious activities are means to attain spiritual growth on our journey.

It is important that we recognize and give thanks for these things and the help they provide in placing and keeping us on the path. Through the spiritual development that teachers and facilities provide, we come closer to God. These are ways and means, but our loyalty must be to God.

REFLECTION

WHEN HAVE YOU LIED TO AN IMPORTANT PERSON IN YOUR LIFE?
HOW DID YOU FIX IT? WHEN HAS AN IMPORTANT PERSON IN YOUR LIFE
LIED TO YOU? WHAT WAS THE OUTCOME?

April 13
Bodily Temptations

The righteous has enough to satisfy his appetite,
but the belly of the wicked suffers want...
Proverbs 13:25

Addictions to anything—drugs, alcohol, possessions, sensuality, whatever it may be—deprive us of the glorious gifts that God wants to provide. These addictions are false gods, and anytime we give in to them, we are not putting God first in our lives.

Prayer, systematic and constant, helps us overcome these temptations and helps us along the spiritual path. The rewards of discipline, faith, and righteous behavior will far exceed momentary pleasures of material things.

Wine is a mocker, strong drink a brawler;
and whoever is led astray by it is not wise.
Proverbs 20:1

REFLECTION

WHAT DOES "IN THE WORLD, BUT NOT OF IT" MEAN TO YOU?

April 14

Vanity

Before destruction a man's heart is haughty,
but humility goes before honor.
Proverbs 18:12

Webster defines personal vanity as excessive pride, conceit. Excessive pride, which can take on many forms, often leads to destruction of one kind or another.

Spiritual pride is the worst form of temptation. It comes to those who have a grasp on part of the truth, yet who are not humble in the truth that they do recognize. When they destroy others with judgmental behavior or a condescending attitude, they put themselves on a path to destruction.

As for man, his days are like grass; he flourishes like a flower of the
field; for the wind passes over it, and it is gone, and its place knows
it no more. But the steadfast love of the Lord is from everlasting to
everlasting upon those who fear him.
Psalm 103:15-16

REFLECTION

LIST THREE PEOPLE YOU ADMIRE. WHY DO YOU ADMIRE THEM?

April 15

Our Challenges, God's Advice, God's Promise

The Lord said to Joshua "…arise…I will not fail you nor forsake you….be strong and of good courage, being careful to do according to all the law…meditate on it day and night…for then you shall be prosperous, and then you shall have good success. Be strong and of good courage…for the Lord your God is with you wherever you go."
Joshua 1:1-9

Moses is dead, and Joshua has been appointed to lead the Israelites into the promised land.

Moses would be a tough act to follow. The path would be a serious challenge.

With all of this facing Joshua, God tells him to meditate on the law both day and night, be strong and of good courage, and that He will be with him. Consider the biggest challenge you face and compare it to succeeding a powerful and popular leader, leading a large tribe of people through the wilderness.

God kept His promise and was present for Joshua. This same promise from the very same unfailing Source is also available to you.

For I am sure that neither death, nor life, nor angels, nor principalities, nor things present, nor things to come, nor powers, nor height, nor depth, nor anything else in all creation, will be able to separate us from the love of God in Christ Jesus our Lord.
Romans 8:38-39

REFLECTION

WHAT OPPORTUNITIES DO YOU SEE
TO CHANGE THE WORLD FOR GOD'S KINGDOM?

April 16

A Just Balance

A just balance and scales are the Lord's;
all the weights in the bag are his.
Proverbs 16:11

Lean in hard to your heavenly Father for strength and hope. Hard times as well as good times are human conditions. They come and go for all of us. God is always the same, and God is always there for us. We may challenge or question this, but the answer is always the same. God loves us totally, completely, and unconditionally, and He wants to bless us.

We limit our ability to accept His blessings when we dwell on the negative of hard times. Likewise, when we accept good times as if we were responsible for creating them, we limit our ability to truly accept and be grateful for what God has given us.

"The aim is to manifest the glory of God in human life,
to live the life hid with Christ in God in human conditions."
Oswald Chambers

REFLECTION

HOW WOULD YOU GRADE YOURSELF IN TERMS OF GRATITUDE?

April 17

Pride and Humility

When pride comes, then comes disgrace;
but with the humble is wisdom.
Proverbs 11:2

Pride can be defined as a great satisfaction resulting from one's own achievements. This is an inward, self-absorbed focus. Self-absorption distracts us from the beauty of others and the world around us. As this scripture indicates, extended periods of self-absorption lead to disgrace. In disgrace, we lose our reputation and the respect of others.

Humility gives love room to grow. The presence of the Holy Spirit removes pride and allows us to focus on others and see their beauty.

For that person must not suppose that a double-minded man,
unstable in all his ways, will receive anything from the Lord.
James 11:1

REFLECTION

WHO DO YOU KNOW THAT CONSISTENTLY EXHIBITS HUMILITY?
WHAT DO YOU THINK OF THAT PERSON?

April 18

He Listens

Because he inclined his ear to me,
therefore I will call on him as long as I live.
Psalm 116:2

One of the best ways to show that we care for others is to listen well. Eye contact and repeating statements for validation indicate that we are listening to what is being said. Also, asking open ended questions (who, when, what, where, why, how, tell me more about…) for further information always improves the communication and gives us deeper understanding of the other person.

The response to this communication is often a similar response back to us. The result can be greater understanding, common ground, further insight, and a better appreciation among children of God.

God is a good listener. He is always there. He is always interested in us and our concerns, and He always cares. God not only listens, He delivers responses. Sometimes we see those responses, sometimes we don't. Sometimes it takes a change in our perspective through prayer, submission, and supplication to understand God's response.

REFLECTION

WHO IN YOUR LIFE NEEDS TO HAVE YOU RESPOND IN LOVE,
NOT ANGER OR INDIFFERENCE?

April 19

Courage

Wait for the Lord; be strong, and let your heart take courage;
yea, wait for the Lord.
Psalm 27:14

The challenges and changes we face, even when the changes are negative, offer us an opportunity for genuine growth. We have all lived through challenges, changes, and disappointing circumstances, but we survived. The real unfortunate outcome from these situations is that we do not always learn the lessons they contain.

When you are on a challenging path, stop for a short period of meditation and reflection. Look for the lessons in your current situation and the possibilities of the path you are on.

REFLECTION

WHEN AND WHY HAVE YOU BEEN AFRAID?
WHAT WAS THE OUTCOME?

April 20

What We Look for We Often Find

He who diligently seeks good seeks favor,
but evil comes to him who searches for it.
Proverbs 11:27

NBA great Bill Russell said, "The game is on the schedule. We have to play it. We might as well win it."

Every situation we encounter is an opportunity to glorify God. Everything is on His schedule. We might as well show up with a winning attitude and expect to win. Regard difficulties as part of the game. Choose to remain positive and prayerful and look for the good in all situations.

Because you have made the Lord your refuge, the Most High your
habitation, no evil shall befall you, no scourge come near your tent.
Psalm 91:9-10

REFLECTION

WHAT OBSTACLES ARE IN YOUR LIFE
THAT KEEP YOU FROM FREEDOM IN CHRIST?

April 21

The Whole Armor

Therefore, take the whole armor of God that you may be able to
withstand in the evil day, and having done all, to stand.
Ephesians 6:13

Be sober, be watchful. Your adversary, the devil,
prowls around like a roaring lion, seeking someone to devour.
1 Peter 5:8

The opportunities for temptation are everywhere. We are constantly in a battle with the adversary. He does not limit the attacks to the typical assumptions of lust and greed. Negative thoughts from fear, doubt, and lack of faith also assault us.

Paul identifies six items of armor for protection in chapter six of his letter to the Ephesians: the belt of truth, the breastplate of righteousness, the boots of the gospel, the shield of faith, the helmet of salvation, and the sword of the Spirit, which is the word of God. All of these point us to "put on the Lord Jesus Christ" (Romans 13:14). This passage reminds us that we have many ways to protect ourselves from temptation and evil. We must have the courage and faith to use them. In the next few devotions, we'll look at each piece of the armor of Christ.

...let us conduct ourselves becomingly as in the day, not reveling
in drunkenness, not in debauchery and licentiousness,
not in quarreling and jealousy.
Romans 13:13

REFLECTION

WHAT DOES IT MEAN TO YOU TO PUT ON THE ARMOR OF GOD?

April 22
The Belt of Truth

Stand therefore, having girded your loins with truth...
Ephesians 6:13

Truth surrounds us. Truth is found in the beauty of creation, its divine and perfect structure of cause and effect, natural sequence, and visual expression. When we cloud our vision with worldly things, we cannot see the truth creation shows us.

Truth is adventure, excitement, and spontaneity that comes with spiritual existence. When we allow our faith to control our thoughts and view each day with gracious uncertainty, these qualities of truth are manifest.

When we open our spiritual eyes, we see that God fills our lives with surprises as He reveals His plan.

Truth is peace, freedom from fear and anxiety, and comfort in the knowledge that God is in control. God's plan is perfect; God's timing is perfect.

Every word of God is true; he is a shield
to those who take refuge in him.
Proverbs 30:5

...you shall have your life as a prize of war,
because you have put your trust in me, says the Lord.
Jeremiah 39:18

REFLECTION

HOW HAS GOD'S DISCIPLINE REFINED AND STRENGTHENED YOU?

April 23

The Breastplate of Righteousness

...and having put on the breastplate of righteousness...
Ephesians 6:14

The breastplate covers the largest area of the body, protecting the heart, lungs, and abdomen. These organs provide blood, air, and nourishment to the rest of the body so other organs can perform their duties.

And so it is, true righteousness protects the person we are and feeds the spirit within us so that we might live in the Lord. True, faithful righteousness provides protection from evil like no other human characteristic.

Jesus taught that the two most important things are loving God with all our being and loving our neighbors as ourselves. Following these two commandments strengthens righteous living.

Trust in the Lord with all your heart, and do not rely on your own insight. In all your ways acknowledge him, and he will make straight your paths.
Proverbs 3:5-6

REFLECTION

WHAT ARE YOU AVOIDING THAT YOU KNOW GOD WANTS YOU TO DO?

April 24

The Boots, Shield, and Helmet

...and having shod your feet with the equipment of the gospel of peace;

*... taking the shield of faith, with which you can quench all
the flaming darts of the evil one. And take the helmet of salvation...*
Ephesians 6:15-17a

The boots, shield, and helmet are all defensive equipment. We can use the gospel of peace, the shield of faith, and the promise of salvation to keep us true to our path in times of adversity and to protect us from the constant assaults of evil that arise in this world.

The constant assaults of evil can often be neutralized by simply ignoring them and allowing our faith to keep us focused on our correct path and the results it will generate.

When these assaults are not neutralized by ignoring them, face them squarely and consider the options and alternatives they offer. There is probably a lesson there or work God wants you to do. Be alert to the assault and stand fast in your faith and convictions.

REFLECTION

WHAT ARE YOUR THREE GREATEST WEAKNESSES?
HOW DO YOU MANAGE THEM?

April 25

The Sword

... and the sword of the Spirit, which is the word of God.
Ephesians 6:17b

The word of God as the sword and prayer are the only weapons of offense mentioned in this reading. The word and prayer are ours to use in battling evil and seeking good. Used consistently and sincerely, they are very effective weapons.

Have no doubt; there is a battle in progress, a cosmic battle between good (God) and evil. Peace will come when there is a cessation of violence between these adversaries, when one side wins and the other submits. The day of battle is every day.

Pray at all times in the Spirit...
Ephesians 6:18

Offense is God's work. We can use the sword—the word of God—and prayer to secure victory over those forces of evil that are assaulting us: greed, lust, doubt, insecurity, fear, anxiety, and any negative thought or feeling that we encounter. We can depend on the promises of God.

REFLECTION

WHAT AREAS OF YOUR LIFE
NEED TO BE SURRENDERED TO GOD'S LORDSHIP?

April 26
Contend on the Side of Good

The horse is made ready for the day of battle,
but the victory belongs to the Lord.
Proverbs 21:31

For we are not contending against flesh and blood, but against the
principalities, against the powers, against the world rulers of this
present darkness, against the spiritual hosts
of wickedness in heavenly places.
Ephesians 6:12

Paul's instructions to the followers of Christ, written while he was a prisoner of the Roman Empire, were prophetic and bold. Though he faced lengthy imprisonment and execution, Paul remained courageous to the end, his faith strong during his lengthy adversity. If we follow his teachings, we will stay true to the faith and contend on the side of good.

Enemies, challenges, and adversities are objects of instruction that offer us opportunities—the opportunity to grow personally or the opportunity to demonstrate and influence others. We do not always know the impact we are having on the lives of others when we face these objects of instruction. Nor do we know the depth and breadth of personal growth we will experience until we deal with them and manage their impact on our future.

REFLECTION

WHAT ENEMIES, CHALLENGES, OR ADVERSITIES ARE YOU FACING RIGHT NOW? WHAT IS YOUR STRATEGY TO OVERCOME THEM?

April 27

Bearing Fruit

...one who sows righteousness gets a sure reward...
Proverbs 11:18

He takes charge of everything. Our part is to walk in the light and obey all that He reveals.

The Spirit of God working in us gives us wisdom. The Christian life is meant to flourish and be vibrant. The fruit we bear comes from the source of our life, not from our own efforts.

The Holy Spirit working in us also captivates others as they see us being doers of the Word, not just bearers.

The fruit of the righteous is a tree of life.
Proverbs 11:30

REFLECTION

HOW HAVE YOUR REGRETS STRENGTHENED YOUR RELATIONSHIP
WITH GOD? WHAT FRUIT CAN YOU SHARE OR SOW TODAY?

April 28

Patience

And we exhort you, brethren, admonish the idlers, encourage the
fainthearted, help the weak, be patient with them all.
1 Thessalonians 5:14

God is more patient with us than we could ever possibly rea-
sonably expect. This is to teach us we are to be patient with
others—certainly not an easy task. However, when we look for the
presence of God in others, having patience with them does become
easier, and we are often blessed as a result.

When patience with others is difficult, we can diffuse the situation by focusing on them as children of God. Thinking of them
in this framework helps us distance ourselves from the obvious
and see the not so obvious sources of their behavior, misbehavior,
moods, or attitudes and thereby possibly see their need.

Let every man be quick to hear, slow to speak, slow to anger,
for the anger of man does not work the righteousness of God.
James 1:19-20

REFLECTION

WHO DO YOU KNOW THAT NEEDS REAL ENCOURAGEMENT NOW?
HOW CAN YOU PROVIDE IT?

April 29

Laugh and the World
Laughs with You

*Then our mouths were filled with laughter, and our tongues
with shouts of joy; then they said among the nations,
"The LORD has done great things for them."*
Psalm 126:2

Laughter is positive, healthy, and contagious. Laughing for ten to fifteen minutes burns up to fifty calories, and raises levels of dopamine and serotonin in the brain, natural chemicals that improve our mood and combat stress and anger.

Spending time with other people increases our opportunities to laugh, and laughing together helps us bond with others. Share your laughter with others!

He will yet fill your mouth with laughter, and your lips with shouting.
Job 8:21

REFLECTION

WHAT THINGS DO YOU THINK MADE JESUS LAUGH?

April 30
Readiness

And he said, "Here am I."
Exodus 3:4

Readiness means a right relationship with God and an awareness of where we are, not where we would like to be—being ready to do whatever we are led to do, even if it seems to be a very small thing.

Being ready is not "getting ready." Being ready means letting go of self and following the teachings of Jesus and the will of God. Letting go of selfishness, jealousy, pride, and all matters of personal gain is challenging but the reward is satisfying and fulfilling.

Humble yourselves therefore under the mighty hand of God, that in due time he may exalt you.
1 Peter 5:6

"After crosses and losses, men grow humbler and wiser."
Benjamin Franklin

REFLECTION

ARE YOU A BELIEVER OR JUST A FAN OF GOD?
WHAT DO YOU THINK IS THE DIFFERENCE?

May 1

Cast the Net

*Jesus said to them, "Cast the net on the right side of the boat,
and you will find some." Their nets filled to the point
that they were not able to haul it in.*
John 21:6

This event takes place after the resurrection when Jesus revealed Himself to the disciples by the Sea of Tiberias. Jesus is standing on the beach as the disciples are fishing. Their nets were empty, and it appeared it would be a fruitless day for fishing. They did not recognize Jesus, and they probably were not expecting him. Then John recognized who it was. "It is the Lord!" he called out in John 21:7.

How often we work with lots of frustration and little result because we are focused on "effort" and not listening to God's voice. God's voice is constant and consistent. When we listen and follow, if we are in the right place, doing the right thing, the results will be right and positive. When we are not listening, doing "our own thing" rather than following, the voice may be telling us to change direction.

Do the right thing because it is the right thing to do.

"Behold, I stand at the door and knock..."
Revelation 3:20

REFLECTION

WHAT DOES "TAKE UP THE CROSS AND FOLLOW JESUS" MEAN TO YOU?

May 2

More Than These

When they had eaten breakfast, Jesus asked Simon Peter, "
Simon, son of John, do you love me more than these?"
John 21:15

It is not totally clear what or who "these" is referring to. As Jesus addresses Peter is He referring to the other disciples? Other people? The fish? Jesus challenges Peter, and us, to focus our love on Him over people or material things.

A deeper question, however, is "Do you trust me?" These are questions that we will be asked.

I love those who love me, and those who seek me diligently find me.
Proverbs 8:17

REFLECTION

WHERE DO YOU PUT CHRIST IN YOUR LIFE?
WHERE DO YOU PLACE YOUR TRUST?

May 3

Simplicity

For a man's ways are before the eyes of the Lord,
and he watches all his paths.
Proverbs 5:21

The Christian life gets simpler. A true Christian will trust the will of God, not his own will. When a person focuses on a purpose of his own, it destroys the simplicity that the children of God can enjoy.

We are to be in communion with God for God's purposes. Events do not happen by chance. They happen for God's purposes and are intended to accomplish His plan.

"...and everything that is written of the Son of man
by the prophets will be accomplished."
Luke 18:31

REFLECTION

HOW DO YOU EXPERIENCE GOD'S PRESENCE?

May 4

Insight and Inspiration

... for we walk by faith, not by sight.
2 Corinthians 5:7

Even in the most difficult of times, God is creating something beautiful. There is always hope, and there is always God's plan, sometimes revealed to us through the perspective that difficulties provide.

We are here as men and women of the world to do God's work. When we are grounded in faith, God provides us with infinite power to endure the turmoil, confusion, and chaos. God gives us glimpses of inspiration when He knows that we are in danger of being led astray.

Therefore do not throw away your confidence, which has a great reward. For you have need of endurance, so that you may do the will of God and receive what is promised.
Hebrews 10: 35-36

REFLECTION

WHAT IS YOUR BIGGEST, MOST PRESSING PROBLEM?
WHAT LESSONS ARE IN THIS PROBLEM?

May 5

Praise Him Always

Then they left the presence of the council, rejoicing that they were
counted worthy to suffer dishonor for the name.
Acts 5:41

Rejoice in moments of suffering for being a witness. This rejoicing helps us make our faith deeper while God does the work with those who created the suffering.

Keeping a positive attitude toward the matters of this world is easier when we adopt a cheerful attitude. The cheerful attitude can be contagious and impacts other people as well as the situation we are involved in. This does not mean a fake cheerfulness but rather a faithful cheerfulness, knowing that God is with us and in the process, we are glorifying Him.

Let your light so shine before men, that they may see your
good works and give glory to your Father who is in heaven.
Matthew 5:16

REFLECTION

WHERE HAVE YOU SEEN POSITIVE RESULTS
GENERATED BY LOVE AND LOVING OTHERS?

May 6

Make a Change

Truly, truly, I say to you, if you ask anything of the Father,
he will give it to you in my name.
John 16:23

If you really want to make a positive change in yourself or your circumstances, God's unlimited power is available, and God wants to help.

Discard self-imposed limitations, negativity, and doubts and build new, positive thoughts. When you have complete faith in God's promises, you can develop personal strength to make those changes.

Consider your challenge. Break it down into its components. Pray for your desired outcome, committing all things to the glory of God. Work on each part of the challenge a step at a time, consciously, steadily, and faithfully. Make prayer and meditation a part of the process to be in tune with God's will. Expect change. You will see improvement, if only in the new habits your efforts generate that are making a stronger, more faithful you.

Remember that this is a spiritual journey. Keep your view positive, be open to the lessons you are to learn, and use this time of reflection and change to strengthen your relationship with God. Be sure to allow forgiveness for yourself as part of this process because God is merciful, and He will forgive you for your shortcomings. Let go of negative emotions and thoughts. Wrap yourself in the love and presence of the Lord and receive what He will give you.

"Ask, and it will be given you; seek, and you will find;
knock, and it will be opened to you."
Matthew 7:7

REFLECTION

HOW DO YOU KNOW WHEN YOU ARE PLEASING GOD?

May 7

What's Stopping You?

Commit your work to the Lord, and your plans will be established.
Proverbs 16:3

…whatsoever you do, do all to the glory of God.
1 Corinthians 10:31

"The shell must break before the bird can fly."
Alfred Lord Tennyson

It has been estimated that a bird pecks at the eggshell 10,000 times before it breaks. By pecking on the shell, the bird is developing neck muscles so it can hold its head up for the next phase of its life—being fed by the mother bird.

We must identify the "shell" that is between us and our true heart's desire. That's where God wants us, that's where we are called according to His purpose. He provided us with that desire, and the talent(s) to accomplish whatever must be done to bring it into our lives according to His purpose. God provides the "shell" to give us the strength to be successful in our next phase.

So, what's stopping you?

Do what is right and do it the right way.

We know that in everything God works for good with those who love him, who are called according to his purpose.
Romans 8:28

REFLECTION

WHAT ARE YOUR AREAS OF DISCONTENT THAT
MAY BE STOPPING YOUR PROGRESS? ARE YOU JEALOUS, ENVIOUS,
OR LACKING IN FAITH? HOW CAN YOU RESPOND DIFFERENTLY?

May 8

Gentle Persuasion

"and I, when I am lifted up from the earth,
will draw all men to myself."
John 12:32

We cannot force others to accept spiritual truth. Our personal peace and understanding will attract them far more quickly than our attempts at convincing with words. Love and respect are gentle persuaders that speak loudly and convince more quickly. Walk and talk in the way of the Lord. Live your own faith journey openly. Be a guide for the others around you to see. Look for and give understanding and patience. Offer an open willing attitude so the love of the Lord in you shines for all to see, regardless of the circumstance you are in.

You never know who is in the audience.

...do it with gentleness and respect.
1 Peter 3:15

REFLECTION

WHAT CRITICISM HAVE YOU RECEIVED RECENTLY?
HOW DID YOU RESPOND? HOW SHOULD YOU RESPOND
IN VIEW OF GOD'S TEACHING?

May 9

Natural Forces

...for you do not know what a day may bring forth.
Proverbs 27:1

When it seems like there is no forward progress, or when your routine is interrupted by disappointment or even discouragement, keep moving prayerfully.

When you witness an airplane taking off, you do not see the million things designed to happen to make the plane ascend, fly, and land at its destination.

Metaphorically, you are traveling in a similar manner. You also were designed to take advantage of natural forces—physical, mental, and spiritual—that enable you to travel through life. When you know your destination and pursue it with prayer and intelligent effort, God's natural forces within you and around you will carry you to your destination.

REFLECTION

HOW, WHEN, AND WHERE
HAVE YOU EXPERIENCED GOD'S PRESENCE RECENTLY?

May 10

Follow Your Passion

The eternal God is your dwelling place,
and underneath are the everlasting arms.
Deuteronomy 33:27

The condition of your life today is the product of your thoughts and choices of your yesterdays. Likewise, the condition of your life tomorrow will be the product of your thoughts and choices today.

If you had an opportunity to enter partnership with the world's most successful person, knowing that their primary interest would be to make sure you were successful, would you accept that opportunity?

You have such an opportunity right now, right where you are, to enter an eternal partnership with God, who created and has dominion over our entire universe and who wants you to be successful.

Do not be conformed to this world but be transformed by the
renewal of your mind, that you may prove what is the will of God,
what is good and acceptable and perfect.
Romans 12:2

REFLECTION

HOW CAN YOU BE MORE RECEPTIVE
TO WHAT GOD WANTS TO PROVIDE FOR YOU?

May 11

Patient Endurance

Because you have kept my word of patient endurance, I will keep you
from the hour of trial which is coming on the whole world...
Revelation 3:10

Faith is confidence, a robust, vigorous confidence, based on the fact that God is Love. When we view the circumstances of this world with patient endurance, accepting God's love for us and these conditions as His—His timing, His purpose, His plan—our lives can become a beautiful romance, full of wonderful opportunities to see His glory in all things all the time.

Now faith is the assurance of things hoped for,
the conviction of things not seen.
Hebrews 11:1

REFLECTION

HOW DOES BEING "A CHILD OF GOD" FEEL TO YOU?
HOW DO YOU RESPOND TO YOUR FATHER?

May 12

Pray for Others

I do not cease to give thanks for you, remembering you in my prayers, that the God of our Lord Jesus Christ, the Father of glory, may give you a spirit of wisdom and of revelation in the knowledge of him, having the eyes of your hearts enlightened, that you may know what is the hope to which he has called you, what are the riches of his glorious inheritance in the saints, and what is the immeasurable greatness of his power in us who believe, according to the working of his great might...

Ephesians 1:16-19

Paul's letter to the Ephesians gives us a wonderful example what Paul prayed about for those in the church at Ephesus. Paul tells the church he prays for them that they will find the hope to which they are called, the riches of God's great inheritance waiting for them, and knowledge of the greatness of God's power.

It is up to them to seek these gifts and accept them according to His will. We can pray lovingly for others, but they must allow God to do the work in their lives.

Long life is in her right hand; in her left hand are riches and honor. Her ways are ways of pleasantness, and all her paths are peace. She is a tree of life to those who lay hold of her; those who hold her fast are called happy.
Proverbs 3:16-18

REFLECTION

HOW DO YOU ACTIVELY PRAY FOR OTHERS?

May 13

Put on Love

And above all these put on love,
which binds everything together in perfect harmony.
Colossians 3:14

When we are faced with several options and must choose one, the correct decision is always the one containing the most love. When we eliminate our personal agenda, submit ourselves to God's will, and approach decisions with prayer, we make ourselves ready for God's answer. "Either or" may become "both and." What seems to be an impossible outcome in our eyes may become a solution easily accomplished when we allow God to show us the way. The way is love, and God is Love.

Put on then, as God's chosen ones, holy and beloved, compassion,
kindness, lowliness, meekness, and patience…
Colossians 3:12

REFLECTION

WHO CAN YOU LOVE TODAY THAT YOU HAVE NEVER LOVED BEFORE?

May 14

Humble Yourself

Humble yourselves before the Lord and he will exalt you.
James 4:10

The "self-made" man or woman is a term that we often use to exalt one who has become successful. Pride is a devastating sin. None of us, no matter how successful in this world's terms, is "self-made."

With each of us, there was the teacher, coach, parent, or friend who put us on the path, who helped us see and develop our own talents. We didn't make ourselves; God made us and provided those special people to give us the direction and support we needed. A saying tells us that when the student is ready, the teacher will appear.

Another bit of wisdom teaches that success is a journey, not a destination. We never finish this journey; we only move forward or backward in accordance with our thought, word, and deed. Our desire should be only to move forward so that, ultimately, God accomplishes through us what He will because we apply faith to our tasks and humility to our self-concept.

You ask and do not receive, because you ask wrongly,
to spend it on your passions.
James 4:3

REFLECTION

WHAT ARE SOME WAYS YOU ARE ATTEMPTING TO BLESS OTHERS?

May 15

In Secret

But when you pray, go into your room and shut the door
and pray to your Father who is in secret;
and your Father who sees in secret will reward you.
Matthew 6:6

Our relationship with God is personal and private. There really are no secrets in this relationship. He knows our innermost desires, our pains, and our pleasures. The more personal and private we allow our prayer to be, the more rewarding our prayer time will become.

When we encounter a problem or conflict, the best remedy is to retreat quickly and completely to God through prayer and meditation. God has the answer. We have only to listen and follow.

...for your Father knows what you need before you ask him.
Matthew 6:8

REFLECTION

HOW WILL YOU PREPARE YOURSELF
TO FOLLOW GOD'S WILL IN THIS COMING DAY?

May 16

At Any Price

Buy truth, and do not sell it; buy wisdom,
instruction, and understanding.
Proverbs 23:23

Truth comes to us when we totally relinquish our own agenda and completely submit to God's will. This is a continuous process. Instruction may come to us in surprising ways when we open our minds and hearts to God's voice. With unconditional love for other people, we see and hear things from them that otherwise we would miss. As we seek understanding, rather than rationalizing our own opinions, we find the fulfilling pleasures that truth and wisdom provide.

The kingdom of heaven is like treasure hidden in a field, which a
man found and covered up; then, in his joy he goes and sells all that
he has and buys that field. Again, the kingdom of heaven is like a
merchant in search of fine pearls, who, on finding one pearl of great
value, went and sold all that he had and bought it.
Matthew 13:44-46

REFLECTION

WHAT HAVE YOU ENCOUNTERED OF GREAT VALUE
IN YOUR FAITH WALK?

May 17

Step Out

Therefore I tell you, do not be anxious about your life, what you shall eat or what you shall drink, nor about your body, what you shall put on. Is not life more than food, and the body more than clothing?
Matthew 6:25

When we become totally dependent upon God and completely release our dependence on things of this world to provide for us, we attain a level of understanding that provides everything we want. If we are secretly looking for someone else to come to our aid or some change of circumstance to provide us with opportunity, we are not totally depending on God.

Step out in faith, knowing that He will provide.

The Lord is the strength of his people...
Psalm 28:8

REFLECTION

NAME ONE WAY YOU WILL STEP OUT TODAY.

May 18
The Effective Life

... make every effort to supplement your faith with virtue, and virtue with knowledge, and knowledge with self-control, and self-control with steadfastness, and steadfastness with godliness, and godliness with brotherly affection, and brotherly affection with love. For if these things are yours and abound, they keep you from being ineffective or unfruitful in the knowledge of our Lord Jesus Christ...
2 Peter 1:5-8

We limit the power of God's love in our lives with self-doubt, negativity, and fear. God's love is ever present, but we will not see or feel it unless we provide an environment to accept it. Faith is essential to having a relationship with God. Supplementing that faith with the elements of virtue, knowledge, self-control, steadfastness, godliness, and agape affection helps us maintain an effective and fruitful relationship. We must work to strengthen these elements in our life to provide the environment necessary to have a fulfilling relationship with God.

His divine power has granted to us all things that pertain to life and godliness...
2 Peter 1:3

REFLECTION

WHAT IS ONE WAY YOU CAN SUPPLEMENT YOUR FAITH?

May 19

Thoughts on Love

... love covers all offenses.
Proverbs 10:11

L ove yourself and others—totally, completely, and unconditionally. Accept the fact that you are totally accepted, just the way
you are. Accept others as you have been accepted.

This requires extreme personal discipline, and it is far easier
to say than do, but this is the path to true contentment, happiness,
and personal productivity. We cannot learn what we are here to
learn and do what we are here to do if we dwell on negative things
or personal weaknesses.

So faith, hope, love abide, these three; but the greatest of these is love.
1 Corinthians 13:13

REFLECTION

WHAT ARE SOME WAYS YOU CAN DEMONSTRATE MERCY THIS WEEK?
WHAT IS ONE NEGATIVE THING YOU CAN LET GO OF TODAY?

May 20

Nine Ways to Love: Part 1

This devotion and the following two offer nine active ways to show love. When we incorporate these actions into our daily lives, we will find richer relationships with those around us and with God as we fulfill His desire for us to love Him and to love one another.

1. **Pay attention to what others say. Listen first, speak last.**

   If one gives answer before he hears, it is his folly and shame.
   Proverbs 18:13

   A fool takes no pleasure in understanding,
   but only in expressing his opinion.
   Proverbs 18:2

2. **Be slow to speak.**

   Let every man be quick to hear, slow to speak, slow to anger...
   James 1:19

3. **Give it like you mean it.**

   ...the righteous gives and does not hold back.
   Proverbs 21:26

REFLECTION

MAKE A NOTE OF WAYS YOU CAN PRAY
FOR EACH MEMBER OF YOUR FAMILY.

May 21

Nine Ways to Love: Part 2

4. **Tell the truth.**

> *Rather, speaking the truth in love, we are to grow up*
> *in every way into him who is the head, into Christ...*
> **Ephesians 4:15**

5. **Pray without ceasing.**

> *...we have not ceased to pray for you, asking that*
> *you may be filled with the knowledge of his will*
> *in all spiritual wisdom and understanding...*
> **Colossians 1:9**

6. **Do not complain.**

> *Do all things without grumbling or questioning...*
> **Philippians 2:14**

REFLECTION

MAKE A NOTE OF WAYS YOU CAN PRAY
FOR EACH PERSON YOU WORK WITH.

May 22

Nine Ways to Love: Part 3

7. **Trust and be trustworthy.**

> *Love bears all things, believes all things, hopes all things,*
> *endures all things.*
> **1 Corinthians 13:7**

8. **Forgive as you have been forgiven.**

> *… forbearing one another and, if one has a complaint against another,*
> *forgiving each other; as the Lord has forgiven you,*
> *so you also must forgive…*
> **Colossians 3:13**

9. **Deliver what you promise.**

> *Hope deferred makes the heart sick,*
> *but a desire fulfilled is a tree of life.*
> **Proverbs 13:12**

> *So faith, hope, love abide, these three; but the greatest of these is love.*
> **1 Corinthians 13:13**

REFLECTION

HOW HAS TIME CHANGED YOUR PERSPECTIVE
ON PEOPLE WHO HURT YOU IN THE PAST?

May 23

The Ultimate Best Relationship

Love is patient and kind; love is not jealous or boastful; it is not arrogant or rude.... Love bears all things, believes all things, hopes all things, endures all things.
I Corinthians 13:4-7

The ultimate best relationship is one in which both parties seek to love, know, and understand God and each other. Recent statistics reveal that:

- 50% of first marriages end in divorce.
- 78% of second marriages end in divorce.
- fewer than 10% of couples who pray together divorce.

These statistics do not represent a lack of love. Factors of this world impact relationships. Factors like greed, selfishness, and poor or nonexistent communication generate hurt feelings. The natural responses to hurt are defensiveness and aggression.

Holy matrimony does not always mean "happy matrimony." Couples that share and grow together in their faith are better equipped to deal with factors of this world, keep them in perspective, and subordinate them to the marriage relationship.

Love never ends.
1 Corinthians 13:8

REFLECTION

WHAT THINGS MAKE YOU WANT TO ARGUE
WITH SOMEONE SIGNIFICANT IN YOUR LIFE? WHY?

May 24

Prayer in Marriage

For where two or three are gathered in my name,
there am I in the midst of them.
Matthew 18:20

Praying together allows both parties to approach God in humble appreciation of His creation.

Our selfish outlook dissipates when we are confronted with God's love and forgiveness. This allows us to forgive each other as we have been forgiven and opens the way for new growth in our relationship. Praying together allows us to expose and address hurt in a safe environment.

Prayer allows us to see possibilities and opportunities for change and embrace unanticipated changes together in the presence of God.

...and the two shall become one flesh. This mystery is a profound one,
and I am saying that it refers to Christ and the church;
however, let each one of you love his wife as himself,
and let the wife see that she respects her husband.
Ephesians 5:31-33

REFLECTION

WHEN WE EXPRESS APPRECIATION BY LISTING THOSE THINGS WE ARE THANKFUL FOR, WHICH PEOPLE, SITUATIONS, AND THINGS ARE ON THE LIST? MORE IMPORTANTLY, WHICH PEOPLE, SITUATIONS, AND THINGS ARE NOT ON THE LIST THAT SHOULD BE?

May 25
Our Relationship

"But by the grace of God I am what I am,
and his grace toward me was not in vain."
1 Corinthians 15:10

The relationship that really matters is our personal relationship with God. When we let everything else become secondary, God will fulfill His purpose through us. When we love as God teaches us, we live in His grace. Human relationships come to us to teach us. Jealousy, envy, and control of others cloud the message. They keep us from learning the lessons and divert our attention from the mission.

When the Spirit of truth comes, he will guide you into all the truth...
John 16:13

REFLECTION

WHAT CAN YOU DO TODAY TO SHARE GOD'S LOVE?

May 26

The Road Ahead

To Thee, O Lord, I call; my rock...
Psalm 28:1

The Lord is my strength and my shield, in him my heart trusts...
Psalm 28:7

In the first verse of Psalm 28, the psalmist seeks protection from his enemies. In verse 7, he recalls the source of his protection.

Was this psalm written during a time of extreme difficulty or did it reflect on that time of difficulty in the past? Does that really matter? God is faithful in everything. When we experience challenges, disappointment, discouragement or hurt, it may be difficult to realize this. However, God's strength and love have not moved away. Have faith.

REFLECTION

**HOW HAVE YOU EXPERIENCED PERSECUTION
IN YOUR DAILY WALK WITH GOD?**

May 27

Go Forward

Five times I have received at the hands of the Jews the forty lashes less one. Three times I have been beaten with rods; once I was stoned. Three times I have been shipwrecked; a night and a day I have been adrift at sea...
2 Corinthians 11:24-25

"I am prepared to go anywhere, provided it be forward."
David Livingstone

Adversity is temporary and so is prosperity. The lessons to be learned are in the midst of each of them. The lessons we learn in these situations are there to prepare us. We do not always know what they are preparing us for, but there is always a purpose.

Paul recounts adversities as events that made him a better witness. He says "...I know a man in Christ who fourteen years ago was caught up..." (2 Corinthians 12:2). Later in verse 10, he says, "...when I am weak, then I am strong." The lessons he learned in experience and adversity enabled him to witness to many and to write words that lead us today.

Dr. David Livingstone, a missionary to Africa, received a message from his missionary society. They asked him to let them know when he had good roads so they could send him people to help him in his work. His response was, "If you have men who will only come if they know there is a good road, I don't want them. I want men who will come if there is no road at all."

...the righteous are bold as a lion.
Proverbs 28:1

REFLECTION

WHEN GOD'S ANSWER TO YOUR PRAYER OR PETITION DID NOT COME IN THE TIME YOU WANTED IT TO, HOW DID YOU RESPOND?

May 28

Be on Guard

For we are not contending against flesh and blood,
but against the principalities, against the powers,
against the world rulers of this present darkness,
against the spiritual hosts of wickedness in the heavenly places.
Ephesians 6:12

Spiritual warfare is constant and consistent. The battle we face is often against powers we do not see, but they fight for control of our consciousness through greed, lust, and the pursuit of pleasures we know are not right.

Paul tells us in his letter to the Ephesians to fight the forces of evil, but we don't have to do it alone. The Holy Spirit is constantly and consistently there to guide us. The battle continues, but the victory is already won.

Immediately upon encountering temptation, negativity, anger, disappointment, anxiety, or any other non-holy thought, turn attention to God and put on His armor.

For, "everyone who calls upon the name of the Lord will be saved."
Romans 10:13

REFLECTION

HOW HAS GOD PROVIDED SPIRITUAL HEALING FOR YOU IN THE PAST?

May 29

He Has No Limits

A Samaritan woman came to draw water, and Jesus said to her,
"Give me a drink." His disciples had gone to the city to buy food. The
Samaritan woman said to him, "How is it that you, a Jew, ask a
drink of me, a woman of Samaria?" For Jews have no dealings with
Samaritans. Jesus answered her, "If you knew the gift of God, and
who it is that is saying to you, 'Give me a drink,' you would have
asked him, and he would have given you living water." The woman
said to him, "Sir, you have no bucket, and the well is deep. Where
do you get that living water? Are you greater than our ancestor Jacob,
who gave us the well, and with his sons and his flocks drank from
it?" Jesus said to her, "Everyone who drinks of this water will be
thirsty again, but those who drink of the water that I will give them
will never be thirsty. The water that I will give will become in them a
spring of water gushing up to eternal life."
John 4:7-14

This account of Jesus and the Samaritan woman has several un-
usual circumstances. Jesus was walking from Judea to Galilee.
He was in Samaria and stopped to rest at Jacob's well. It was "about
the sixth hour," which is about noon and He was alone for the
moment as the disciples had gone away into the city to buy food.
Although it was the custom of women to collect water at the well
early in the day, on this day a Samaritan woman came to the well
at noon. The story explains that it was not the custom for Jews and
Samaritans to share things, yet Jesus asked her for a cup of water,
violating the political and social custom.

The Samaritan woman heard his request with surprise and did
not immediately perceive there was a deeper message. Upon hearing the further words from Jesus, she began to understand what

He was telling her and ran to tell others of His message about the living water. You can read the rest of the story in John 4:15-30.

How often do we look at a situation from our limited, human perspective and not see the deeper meaning? We look at matters of this world and see things only superficially from our own needs and wants. What if we took time to consider the greater need, the greater joy, the more beautiful path of searching for God's will?

REFLECTION

**WHAT HAVE YOU LEARNED FROM THOSE
WHO DISAGREE WITH YOU OR PERSECUTE YOU?**

May 30
Let God Do the Work

But Jesus looked at them and said to them, "With men this is
impossible, but with God all things are possible."
Matthew 19:26

...he who makes haste with his feet misses his way.
Proverbs 18:2

We do not "help" God; God helps us. God offers us the opportunity to do His work through us. God will fulfill His word, and He will keep His promises.

Patience in the face of doubt, persistence in times of difficulty, and prayer at all times are the guideposts of the roads we travel. His work is not always the work that seems to be most logical to us, but we are called to abide by His plan and His timing and do what He wants us to do.

REFLECTION

WHAT DO YOU LEARN FROM WAITING?

May 31

In Challenging Times

...I do as the Father has commanded me,.... Rise, let us go hence.
John 14:31

Jesus is talking to eleven of His disciples. He has dismissed Judas with "What you are going to do, do quickly" (John 13:27). He knows that His crucifixion is near, and He is fully aware of what it will accomplish. Some of His most memorable comments come from this address as He thinks of others.

In John 14:1 *"Let not your heart be troubled..."*

In John 14:12 *"...he who believes in me will also do the works that I do; and greater works..."*

In John 14:27 *"Peace I leave with you..."*

In John 15:5 *"I am the vine, you are the branches..."*

When we are going through challenging times, times of trial or extreme difficulty, we are not usually aware of—or even thinking about—our impact on others. It is during hard times that we must accept our duty and act in faith that God brings all to His good. This will bring peace to our soul and be a light to others who may be observing our words and actions. We never know—our impact on others may be immediate or it may be eternal.

REFLECTION

**HOW HAVE YOU EXPERIENCED A FEELING
OF BEING INSIGNIFICANT AT WORK OR AT HOME?**

June 1

Criticism: Constructive or Otherwise

Better is a dry morsel with quiet than a house
full of feasting with strife.
Proverbs 17:1

A cheerful heart is good medicine,
but a downcast spirit dries up the bones.
Proverbs 17:22

Nothing is accomplished by criticism. Criticism disperses the spirit of the one criticized. Suggestions and comments offered in loving concern are a different matter. Proper wording, voice tonality, and expression can communicate that loving concern. If love is not the intent, it is best to remain quiet.

Let no evil talk come out of your mouth,
but only such as is good for edifying, as fits the occasion, that it may
impart grace to those who hear.
Ephesians 4:29

Therefore you have no excuse, O man, whoever you are,
when you judge another; for in passing judgment upon him
you condemn yourself...
Romans 2:1

REFLECTION

WHEN YOU OFFER CRITICISM, WHAT IS YOUR INTENT?
HOW DO YOU OFFER CRITICISM?

June 2

Our Counselors

...for by wise guidance you can wage your war,
and in abundance of counselors there is victory.
Proverbs 24:6

Where do we find counselors? Everywhere. There are those who are highly trained whose gifts are in counseling others. They provide special blessings to those who seek and follow their guidance. This is especially true when both counselor and those being counseled seek wisdom and truth from God.

God also places others along our paths who are not so highly trained but who were placed to deliver His messages. God is constantly speaking to us through circumstances, "signs and wonders," and other people. We can hear His voice as we learn to depend on God's wisdom and not our own through what and who He sends us.

I, wisdom, dwell in prudence and I find knowledge in discretion.
Proverbs 8:12

I (wisdom) love those who love me,
and those who seek me diligently find me.
Proverbs 8:17

REFLECTION

WHOM WOULD YOU CHOOSE TO BE YOUR MENTOR? WHY?

June 3

Go for It!

... the righteous are bold as a lion.
Proverbs 28:1

Our dreams, our desires, our passions are all there for a reason. Most likely, they are to guide us along the path that ultimately leads to accomplishing God's plan for us.

When we doubt ourselves, when we carry guilt over our shortcomings and sins (refusing to accept God's grace), we limit God's influence in our lives. We cannot accomplish the things God has planned for us when we carry a load of guilt and doubt.

Inventory your dreams, write down your desires, identify your passions, and thank God for all of them. Then go for them boldly, knowing who is leading you, who is beside you every step, and who is waiting for you at the finish line.

Don't look for your dreams to come true; instead, look to become true to your dreams.

When the righteous triumph, there is great glory.
Proverbs 28:12

REFLECTION

WHAT CONFLICTS DO YOU HAVE IN YOUR LIFE
THAT WOULD BE IMPROVED WITH SPIRITUAL DIRECTION?
WHAT STEPS CAN YOU TAKE TO BE TRUE TO YOUR DREAM?

June 4
Self-Confidence

Be still before the Lord and wait patiently for him; fret not yourself over him who prospers in his way...
Psalm 37:7

And let us not grow weary in well-doing, for in due season we shall reap, if we do not lose heart.
Galatians 6:9

Shortcuts create a path of disappointment. Honesty, integrity, and working hard at doing the right things the right way ultimately will lead to the best outcomes for all concerned.

It's all practice. Do not expect perfect results, but continue to practice in faith and confidence, drawing near to God and living in righteous behavior. We are all here to learn. Whether we encounter disappointment, difficulty, or discouragement or we experience victory or triumph, there are valuable lessons to learn. What we learn prepares us for future experiences along God's path for us.

Ultimately, we are totally, completely, and unconditionally acceptable to God. Our quality of life is proportional to our response to circumstances. We can accept, learn, and move on, or we can resent and regret and stay in place.

The fruit of the righteous is a tree of life.
Proverbs 11:30

REFLECTION

DO YOU REASON WITH GOD IN YOUR PRAYERS AND PETITIONS? WHY OR WHY NOT?

June 5

Start with Peace

Peace I leave with you; my peace I give to you; not as the world gives
do I give to you. Let not your hearts be troubled,
neither let them be afraid.
John 14:27

Jesus is speaking to His disciples following the last supper. He knows what is about to happen to Him. ("...the hour is coming...." John 16:25.) There will be blasphemous persecution by religious leaders, public mocking by people of this world, extreme physical pain in the worst type of execution known at the time, and death—yet His message is that He is at peace and He is delivering that same peace to them, a peace that surpasses all human understanding.

With these words, Jesus implies that the gift of peace, peace of mind and freedom from fear, is the greatest of all God's gifts. Peace of mind is one of the most important things anyone can possess. Without it, all other things assume far too much importance. With it, everything takes its proper position and proportion.

These things I have spoken to you, that my joy may be in you,
and that your joy may be full.
John 15:11

REFLECTION

HOW DO YOU HANDLE STRESS? HOW COULD YOU IMPROVE THE
PROCESS? HOW CAN YOU ADD MORE PEACE TO YOUR LIFE?

June 6

Cheer Up!

A glad heart makes a cheerful countenance.
Proverbs 15:13

Sometimes we don't understand an experience at the time we are living it. The experience is preparing us. Whatever we are being prepared for is part of God's plan, and His ultimate plan for us is full of joy, happiness, and fulfillment. Now is a time to be filled with gladness, regardless of current circumstances, because we know the joy of the "continual feast" is ahead of us.

A cheerful heart has a continual feast.
Proverbs 15:15

REFLECTION

HOW WOULD YOU FEEL IF TOMORROW YOU WOKE UP
AND DISCOVERED THAT YOU HAD LOST EVERYTHING
YOU WERE NOT THANKFUL FOR TODAY?

June 7
Build on a Rock

*Everyone then who hears these words of mine and does them will be
like a wise man who built his house upon the rock...*
Matthew 7:24

The nature of spiritual life is that we are certain in our uncertainty.

Leave it all to God and find comfort even in the uncertainty of what He will do, knowing that He will reveal what we need to know when, and if, we need to know. He is carrying out His plan. Parts of it may not make sense to us, but His plan is greater than we can possibly comprehend. We participate and contribute best when we pray, accept, and follow in gracious uncertainty.

Life sometimes sends us unexpected storms. We cannot always control events, but we can build strong foundations. A foundation built on the rock of a personal relationship with God does not allow us to control events, but it does enable us to control our responses with the strength of our faith.

*Beloved, we are God's children now;
it does not yet appear what we shall be...*
1 John 3:2

REFLECTION

**DURING TIMES OF CHALLENGE, CHANGE, OR STRESS,
HOW HAS GOD HELPED YOU?**

June 8

Outward Appearance and Influence

Sing to the Lord, bless his name…
Psalm 96:2

Whether we like it or not, the world judges us by our outward appearance and behavior. What we say and how we say it communicates who we are and what we believe.

Jesus projected joy, confidence, and peace that made Him attractive to crowds and influenced the lives of thousands. We can have a similar experience when we accept His love and share it earnestly through our outward behavior.

Worship the Lord in holy array…
Psalm 96:9

REFLECTION

HOW DO YOU USE THE GIFTS GOD GAVE YOU
TO COMMUNICATE WITH THOSE AROUND YOU?

June 9
In Everything God Works for Good!

We know that in everything God works for good with those
who love him, who are called according to his purpose.
Romans 8:28

For the next three days, do not allow yourself to dwell on any kind of negative thought. Watch yourself closely and carefully and do not under any circumstances allow negative thoughts to remain in place. Instead, quickly replace them with constructive, positive, optimistic, kind, and loving thoughts.

Do not assume this will be an easy task. The discipline may be very strenuous, but after three days, you may see a habit of positive thinking begin to emerge and positive changes begin to come into your life. Feel encouraged by this new way of looking at and receiving what life brings. Your mentality will begin to automatically align with your new outlook, and you will find new peace and joy even in hard times. Continue the practice!

REFLECTION

WHY DO YOU THINK IT IS SO DIFFICULT TO GIVE UP BAD HABITS?

June 10

A Love Letter from Paul

So faith, hope, love abide, these three; but the greatest of these is love.
1 Corinthians 13: 13

God has many gifts to give, but the greatest and most abiding one is love. The gift of love we receive is greatest when we share it with others...all others.

Loving and serving others has its own reward. When we love and serve others, they often want to respond in kind by loving and serving others themselves. Even if they do not, the reward is still there for us. The real pleasure comes from loving, not necessarily being loved by, others.

And a new commandment I give to you, that you love one another; even as I have loved you, that you also love one another.
John 13:34

REFLECTION

HOW DOES THE NEWS OF TODAY
CONTRAST WITH WHAT GOD'S NEWS IS TELLING YOU?

June 11

Quiet Confidence

In quietness and confidence shall be your strength.
Isaiah 30:15

We are afflicted in every way, but not crushed; perplexed, but not driven to despair; persecuted, but not forsaken; struck down, but not destroyed; always carrying in the body the death of Jesus, so that the life of Jesus may also be manifested in our bodies.
2 Corinthians 4:8-9

In spiritual work, effort defeats itself. When we try to hurry spiritual work, when we force things, the power dissipates or even disappears. When we are unhurried, gentle, and faithful, we allow God to do the work through us.

Quiet confidence is our reflection of God's presence in our lives. Quiet confidence comes when we focus on His presence, listen for His voice, and look for His presence in other people.

Let go and let God do His work.

The plans of the diligent lead surely to abundance,
but everyone who is hasty comes only to want.
Proverbs 21:5

REFLECTION

TAKE THIS OPPORTUNITY TO REFLECT ON AN OUTSTANDING EVENT IN YOUR LIFE. THINK OF A TIME THAT WAS VERY SPECIAL WHEN YOU WERE AT YOUR BEST. WHAT STRENGTHS WERE YOU FEELING? DESCRIBE HOW YOU FELT IN EVERY SENSORY WAY YOU CAN. HOW DID IT FEEL? WHAT SOUNDS, SMELLS, AND SIGHTS DO YOU RECALL?

June 12

Love is Spontaneous

Love is patient and kind; love is not jealous or boastful...
Proverbs 13:4

Love's source is in God. We can love because God first loved us and gave us the ability to love. Indeed, God calls upon us to love Him and to love our brothers and sisters.

As we embrace this way to live with the Spirit of God in us, things of this world lose their attractiveness. This nature of love is visible to others in our actions and attitude, and it can be contagious. We become instruments of God's love.

God's love has been poured into our hearts through
the Holy Spirit which has been given to us.
Romans 5:5

REFLECTION

HOW DO YOU BEST CONNECT WITH GOD?

June 13

The Hope of the Righteous

The hope of the righteous ends in gladness.
Proverbs 10:28

God's presence is always available to those who believe. God's presence is the source of full and lasting pleasure. All we have to do is seek, believe, and receive. Prayer helps us to focus our thoughts. Adding positive, happy thoughts of thanksgiving and praise will make us more receptive to God's word and will please Him. Be glad in the time you spend with God.

How lovely is Thy dwelling place, O Lord of hosts!
My soul longs, yea, faints for the courts of the Lord;
my heart and flesh sing for joy to the living God.
Psalm 84:1-2

REFLECTION

HOW DO YOU SEE GOD AS THE SOURCE OF BEAUTY?

June 14

A Day of Rest

*So God blessed the seventh day and hallowed it, because on it
God rested from all his work which he had done in creation.*
Genesis 2:3

God blessed and hallowed a time of rest. Time of rest, after the work is done, is a blessed gift from God. When we set aside time for rest, reflection, and recovery from the day-to-day world, we can find renewal and peace.

Slow down, spend time meditating, listening, and thanking God for this gift of rest.

*...he makes me lie down in green pastures.
He leads me beside still waters; he restores my soul.*
Psalm 23:2-3

REFLECTION

DO YOU HAVE A HABIT OF DAILY MEDITATION?
IF YES, HOW DOES IT REWARD YOU? IF NOT, WHY NOT?

June 15

Human Beings or Human Doings?

He only is my rock and my salvation, my fortress...
Psalm 62:2

When you feel like your life is out of control, stop! Turn to God! This is a time to meditate, pray, and listen. Let God in. Employees spend 25% of their time doing urgent but unimportant tasks. The percentage might be greater in our personal lives. When we are overwhelmed, we should stop and look at what we are doing and ask ourselves these questions:

- Is this really important?
- What would be the result if this was not done?
- What is the result I am trying to generate?
- Could this be done more effectively a different way?

The Pareto Principle that says 20% of what we do generates 80% of the results can be applied to most situations in work and in life. Taking the time to realize God's presence in everything we do will transfigure our tasks as well as ourselves.

He who makes haste with his feet misses his way.
Proverbs 19:2

REFLECTION

HOW DOES GOD FIT IN YOUR SCHEDULE?

June 16
The Buffalo Paradox

When you pass through the waters I will be with you; and through the rivers, they shall not overwhelm you; when you walk through fire you shall not be burned and the flame shall not consume you.
Isaiah 43:2

Author Rory Vaden (*Take the Stairs: 7 Tips to Achieving True Success*) recalls a lesson from nature in his home state of Colorado. In Colorado, the plains roll from the foothills of the Rocky Mountains toward the east. Because of the unique topography and climate, this is one of a few places in the world that has both buffalo and cows.

When a storm approaches from the west, cows know the storm is coming, so they head east in an effort to outrun the storm. Cows are not very fast. When the storm comes, they continue to proceed in the same direction at their slow pace, and the result is a lengthy exposure to the storm's conditions.

The buffalo, knowing that the storm is coming, wait for the storm to arrive, then turn and charge directly into it, minimizing their time of exposure. There is a lesson to learn from the buffalo about facing our troubles.

Whatever our difficulties, whatever problems we encounter, God is in the midst of them. God will be with us always to help us resolve them.

REFLECTION

WHAT HAS BEEN THE MOST DIFFICULT TIME IN YOUR LIFE?
HOW DID YOU RECOVER?

June 17

Look Where You Are Going

To thee I lift up my eyes, O thou who art enthroned in the heavens! Behold, as the eyes of servants look to the hand of their master, as the eyes of a maid to the hand of her mistress, so our eyes look to the Lord our God till he have mercy upon us...
Psalm 123:1-2

Whatever you think about, whatever you really concentrate on and truly believe, will be manifest in your life.

Look where you are going, because you will go where you are looking.

Our daily walk with God is full of challenges, some divine, some man-made, and some of evil origin. When trouble comes to us, when we misstep, we can look to the Lord with faith and confidence in His mercy.

...a good person will be filled with the fruit of his deeds.
Proverbs 14:14

REFLECTION

HOW WOULD YOU DESCRIBE THE FRUIT YOU ARE BEARING?

June 18

Expectation and Anticipation

...in quietness and in trust shall be your strength.
Isaiah 30:15

Leaders who embrace change and creatively manage its impact on the future are often viewed as visionary and self-confident. This is by far the most effective way to lead others and inspire confidence. The only constant is change. Change causes discomfort among most followers, but when they see the leader embrace and welcome change, it diminishes their discomfort. In fact, good leaders facilitate creative response to change which enables their followers to participate in embracing and managing its impact.

When we conduct ourselves, our relationships, and our day-to-day activities according to God's principles and when we trust His strength, we can notice Him working in great and unexpected ways. We are on the path to spiritual maturity when we give all power to God, truly believe that prayer can do anything, and expect to see God's presence everywhere.

Draw near to God and he will draw near to you.
James 4:8

REFLECTION

WHAT ARE THE GREATEST TRIUMPHS YOU HAVE EXPERIENCED?
HOW DID YOU RESPOND?

June 19

Miracles Can—and Do—Happen

Keep your heart with all vigilance, for from it flow the springs of life.
Proverbs 4:23

But Jesus beheld them and said unto them, "With men this is impossible; but with God all things are possible."
Matthew 19:26

The Bible tells us repeatedly that miracles can happen. It even gives detailed accounts of many specific miracles. Miracles can happen if you believe them to be possible and if you are willing to recognize God's power and call on Him.

Look for miracles!

Miracles are real. Things do happen that we cannot otherwise explain.

REFLECTION

WHAT DO YOU THINK A MIRACLE LOOKS LIKE?

June 20

Silence is a Gift

*...when I think of thee upon my bed, and meditate on thee
in the watches of the night...*
Psalm 63:6

God speaks to us constantly, yet we often miss His communication due to the noise of this world.

We are so preoccupied with the methods of mass communication and media that messages of this world consume our time and control our thoughts.

Just a few minutes of silence and meditation can cause dramatic shifts in our attitude and can actually cause positive physical changes in our bodies.

REFLECTION

HOW DO YOU RECOGNIZE THE SHEPHERD'S VOICE?

June 21

Wisdom

The beginning of wisdom is this: Get wisdom,
and whatever you get, get insight.
Proverbs 4:7

Webster defines wisdom as "understanding of what is true, right, or lasting."

Proverbs 8:1-3 tell us that wisdom is calling out to us from all directions, all the time: "on the heights, in the paths, beside the gates, at the entrance of the portals...."

The act of seeking wisdom and understanding is the basis of spiritual growth. We are all on this journey, and we move at our own pace. No one is "in front" of us; no one is "behind us." Those who are earnestly seeking Wisdom will hear, see, or feel its presence. The voice, vision, or feeling is consistent and constant. The clarity with which we hear, see, or feel this presence increases with our efforts of faith and meditation.

I love those who love me, and those who seek me diligently find me.
Proverbs 8:17

REFLECTION

WHAT DOES IT MEAN TO YOU TO BE
LIVING AUTHENTICALLY IN WISDOM?

June 22

Detours

A man's mind plans his way, but the LORD directs his steps.
Proverbs 16:9

G od directs our steps, even when we plan. When our path is obstructed or our journey is interrupted by detours, it is God's direction that causes these changes in our plans. These changes and interruptions happen for a reason, God's reason.

These divine interruptions to our routine are there to teach us. When they are particularly challenging, there may be a lesson to learn that will change the direction of our lives. When they seem simple, there may be an opportunity to see something or someone that will expand our consciousness of the glory of God's creation.

REFLECTION

WHAT DETOURS DO YOU SEE RIGHT NOW IN YOUR LIFE?
WHY DO YOU THINK THEY ARE THERE?

June 23

His Answers

The fear of the Lord is the beginning of wisdom,
and the knowledge of the Holy One is insight.
Proverbs 9:10

God reveals Himself to us following our obedience. We cannot learn what God is telling us solely through study, reading, or analysis. When we trust and listen, obedience clears the channel.

God is speaking to us all the time, directly or indirectly. Unfortunately, we are often distracted by things of this world, and we don't hear His voice because of the noise the world creates. Make time in your day to be with God, to sit in silence and awe, to study a scripture passage, to petition, to give thanks—to get to know God better.

REFLECTION

DESCRIBE TRUE CONTENTMENT.
HOW DOES THIS APPLY TO YOUR CURRENT ATTITUDE?

June 24

Have Patience

For thus said the Lord, the Holy one of Israel, "In returning and rest
you shall be saved; in quietness and in trust shall be your strength."
Isaiah 30:15

Relaxed, unhurried concentration often generates results that impatience and hurried activity would not. When we relax and look at "the big picture," we often see things that we would not otherwise see.

Focus on process rather than results. Let God guide you through the process, then evaluate the potential results from a positive perspective. Forget "we always do it this way."

Prior to the 1968 Olympic Games, the high jump was accomplished with a head-on or scissors jumping process. Commentators joked about the funny backwards style of American athlete Dick Fosbury—until he won the Gold Medal. Today, the "Fosbury flop" is the dominant high jump procedure. Fosbury took a new way with confidence.

Travel your path with confidence in God, take your time, don't be fearful of doing something "different" if that is what you are called to do.

The plans of the diligent lead surely to abundance,
but everyone who is hasty comes only to want.
Proverbs 21:5

REFLECTION

WHAT IMPORTANT LESSON DO YOU HAVE TO SHARE
FROM YOUR LIFE'S EXPERIENCES?

June 25

The Cost of Obedience

*For which of you, desiring to build a tower, does not first sit down
and count the cost, whether he has enough to complete it?*
Luke 14:28

Our spiritual growth is reflected in our attitude toward obedience. The reward is great, but the cost is dear. Jesus was hated by some, challenged by many, and ignored by most. We may experience the same cost when we follow Him.

Obedience certainly involves denying the temptations of the world, but it also involves right thinking. Right thinking may result in changed or severed relationships, loss of status, or even being mistreated by those we think of as friends.

Jesus advises us to calculate the cost and determine whether we have enough to complete the journey. However, He also shares the load when we commit to the journey.

*And your ears shall hear a word behind you, saying, "This is the way,
walk in it," when you turn to the right or when you turn to the left.*
Isaiah 30:21

REFLECTION

WHAT IS THE MOST IMPORTANT THING
YOU CAN MAKE HAPPEN THIS WEEK?

June 26

Purpose and Prayer

Our circumstances today are a result of our choices yesterday. Unfortunately, our choices are rarely perfect. However, when our choices result in a problem, there is usually a lesson to learn.

Our duty in these situations is to learn the lesson and grow.

Don't try to explain away a decision that did not work well or a mistake. Accept the responsibility. Denial only delays any positive action we can take if correction is needed. Ask God for a positive perspective in the situation and for the momentum to move forward on the right path.

Know that God is there. We must forget what has happened and focus on what we are going to make happen. Then, give it our best effort.

Many are the plans in the mind of a man,
but it is the purpose of the LORD that will be established.
Proverbs 19:21

REFLECTION

WHAT IS THE MOST IMPORTANT THING
SOMEONE ELSE IS EXPECTING FROM YOU TODAY?

June 27

Practice

Be ye doers of the word, and not hearers only...
James 1:22

"Practice is the best of all instructors."
Publilius Syrus

Practice is the price of proficiency. There are few notable accomplishments that do not require practice. The more we practice, the more proficient we become. This is true in human endeavors, and we all have seen good examples.

This is particularly true when we practice at being in the presence of God. When we practice being and remaining in a faith-filled state of cheerful expectancy, we realize His presence more powerfully. God is always there, and with practice, we grow in our own awareness of Him—in others, in the world about us, and in ourselves.

REFLECTION

WHAT IS THE MOST IMPORTANT THING YOU WILL DO TODAY?

June 28

Listen

...he who listens to me will dwell secure and will be at ease...
Proverbs 1:33

Moments of inspiration are special. We are here to do work in the world, and when we listen to God, we do that work to His glory. Occasionally, God provides special moments when we need them the most. However, these moments are rare. We must walk by faith most of the time. Then, upon reflection, we find that God was there all the time.

...for we walk by faith, not by sight.
1 Corinthians 5:7

REFLECTION

IN THOSE TIMES WHEN GOD SEEMS TO BE FAR AWAY,
HOW DO YOU RESPOND?

June 29

Bearing Fruit

...a good person will be filled with the fruit of his deeds.
Proverbs 14:14

Proverbs does not say it in the passage above, but the corollary of this text applies to the "bad" person. In either case, the person reaps what is sowed. Good fruit from good things, bad fruit from bad things. Unfortunately, it sometimes appears that those who sow bad seeds reap good fruit—at least temporarily. Even if that happens, it is not our concern. God's mercy and justice will ultimately prevail in ways and times we never see.

And let us not grow weary in well doing, for in due season
we shall reap, if we do not lose heart.
Galatians 6:9

...the fruit of the Spirit is love, joy, peace, patience, kindness,
goodness, faithfulness, gentleness, self-control...
Galatians 5:22

But, as it is written, "what no eye has seen, nor ear heard, nor the heart of man conceived, what God has prepared for those who love him," God has revealed to us through the Spirit.
1 Corinthians 2:9-10

REFLECTION

HOW DO YOU DESCRIBE "WALKING IN THE FAITH?"

June 30

Handling Anxiety

Humble yourselves therefore under the mighty hand of God...
1 Peter 5:6

There are wonderful things taking place in areas we do not see. They will be revealed in due time, in God's time. Consider any of the wonders of the world around us. When we view a plant, we cannot see the growth that is occurring inside the plant to generate flowers in their due season. When we look at a hen sitting on an egg, there is a lot happening inside that egg that we cannot see, but in due season, it will hatch and a new life will be revealed.

God's outcome is mighty. Praise His works and commit yourself to His plan. He is at work in you.

Commit your work to the Lord, and your plans will be established.
Proverbs 16:3

REFLECTION

TAKE TIME TO RECALL AN EVENT OR SET OF CIRCUMSTANCES IN THE
PAST THAT CAUSED A HIGH LEVEL OF ANXIETY FOR YOU.
DESCRIBE THE EVENT OR CIRCUMSTANCES IN AS MUCH DETAIL
AS YOU CAN. NOW, LOOK AT THE EVENT OR CIRCUMSTANCES
FROM TODAY'S PERSPECTIVE. WHAT WAS THE LESSON?
WHAT DID YOU LEARN? HOW DID YOU GROW?

July 1
God Owns It—We Manage It

Thine, O LORD, is the greatness, and the power, and the glory,
and the victory, and the majesty; for all that is in the heavens
and in the earth is thine; thine is the kingdom, O LORD,
and thou art exalted as head above all.
1 Chronicles 29:11

The Chronicler is quoting King David. The people have given willingly and freely to the construction of the temple, the house of the Lord, and he rejoices with them.

"My" is a word we consistently misuse. My house, my money, my job express ownership that connotes entitlement. We often carry it even further with "my accomplishments, my success, my—, my—, my—"

We need to have a mentality toward assets and accomplishments that reflects their true source.

God has entrusted us with those possessions and talents. King David understood this, communicated it, and lived it though he was not perfect.

For all things come from thee, and of thy own have we given thee.
1 Chronicles 29:14

REFLECTION

HOW CAN YOU BETTER SHARE "OWNERSHIP"
IN YOUR LIFE WITH GOD?

July 2

What We Say

A fool's lips bring strife, and his mouth invites a flogging.
A fool's mouth is his ruin, and his lips are a snare to himself.
Proverbs 18: 6-7

It is always better to keep our thoughts private until the appropriate time to reveal them. We are all guilty of talking too much, speaking too soon, and hurting others without meaning to. Silence can provide a very powerful comment.

Make your words soft and sweet because you never know when you may have to eat them.

Even a fool who keeps silent is considered wise;
when he closes his lips, he is deemed intelligent.
Proverbs 17:28

REFLECTION

WHO IN YOUR DAILY LIFE NEEDS TO HEAR
THE GOOD NEWS OF THE GOSPEL?

July 3

The Time Is Right

Besides this you know what hour it is, how it is full time now for you to wake from sleep. For salvation is nearer to us now than when we first believed; the night is far gone, the day is at hand. Let us then cast off the works of darkness and put on the armor of light...
Romans 13:11-12

God is ready when you are. There is nothing to wait for, nothing to change but your mind. Do not keep yourself out of the Kingdom by finding reasons to postpone.

God's time for your demonstration is right now! The time God wants you to be healed is now! The time God wants you to be in the true place He has for you is now! The time to be happy is now! The place to be happy is here!

Talk does not cook rice.
Chinese proverb

REFLECTION

WHAT ARE THE BELIEFS AND CONVICTIONS
YOU WOULD BE WILLING TO TAKE PUNISHMENT FOR?

July 4
Who Does the Work?

I planted, Apollos watered, but God gave the growth. So neither he who plants nor he who waters is anything, but only God who gives the growth. He who plants and he who waters are equal, each shall receive his wages according to his labor. For we are God's fellow workers; you are God's field, God's building.
1 Corinthians 3:6-9

As workers, we should have one concern: to concentrate on God. Once the concentration is on God, all other matters in life fall into place. Our responsibility is to remain in touch with God and see that we allow nothing to interfere. God will engineer everything. Wherever He puts us is where we are to show our total devotion to His will and our wholehearted devotion to Him in the work He has given us to do.

Whatever your hand finds to do, do it with your might...
Ecclesiastes 9:10

REFLECTION

HOW CAN YOU DISPLAY GOD'S GLORY IN YOUR WORK?

July 5
What Is God Like?

The Lord is near to all who call upon him, to all who
call upon him in truth.
Psalm 145:18

God is Spirit, and those that worship him must worship
in spirit and in truth.
John 4:24

To worship God in spirit requires gaining a spiritual understanding of His nature. To define God in the traditional sense
would indicate that there are limits to God. God has no limits in
time or space, no boundaries of any kind. However, there are many
aspects of God, and seven of them are revealed to us as very important. These primary aspects are fundamental truths about the
nature of God, truths that never change. God is Life, Light, Truth,
Love, Intelligence, Spirit, and Principle. Over the next seven days
we will explore these aspects in more depth.

But the hour is coming, and now is, when the true worshipers
will worship the Father in spirit and in truth,
for such the Father seeks to worship him.
John 4:23

God has revealed to us through the Spirit.
For the Spirit searches everything, even the depths of God.
1 Corinthians 2:10

REFLECTION

WHAT THINGS, ACTIVITIES, OR PEOPLE
ARE COMPETING WITH YOUR DEVOTION TO GOD?

July 6

God Is Life

Jesus said to him, "I am the Way, the Truth, and the Life..."
John 14:6

Thou dost show me the paths of life; in Thy presence there is fullness of joy, in Thy right hand are pleasures for evermore.
Psalm 16:11

Jesus tells us that those who follow Him shall have the light of life. You experience this light of life when you feel joyous, free of fear, and free of doubt. Your life is a consecrated life when you are always ready to do the will of God. Your thoughts, words, and deeds show it. God will provide the results when you remain focused on His word and seek His will.

Keep your heart with all vigilance; for from it flow the springs of life.
Proverbs 4:23

REFLECTION

**WHY DO YOU THINK GOD ENTERED OUR LIVES
AS A MAN, JESUS CHRIST?**

July 7
God is Light

...God is light and in him is no darkness at all.
1 John 1:5

Light changes the things we see and the way we see them. Selfishness, doubt, fear, and anxiety darken our view and obscure the truth. When we remove selfishness, doubt, fear, and anxiety and look to God with faith, hope, and love, we see things in true light as they really are.

...for once you were darkness, but now you are light in the Lord;
walk as children of light (for the fruit of the Light is found
in all that is good and right and true)...
Ephesians 5:8-9

REFLECTION

WHERE DO YOU NEED TO SHINE MORE LIGHT?

July 8

God is Truth

...and you will know the truth, and the truth will make you free.
John 8:32

Truth does not change. Truth in any matter—love, sport, relationships with others, or business dealings—does not change. What is true remains true. When we try to "spin" it, change it, or deny it, we only lead ourselves and others astray. Ultimately, the truth must surface. When it does surface, all things fall into their proper place.

REFLECTION

WHAT DOES LIVING WITH HONESTY AND INTEGRITY MEAN TO YOU?

July 9
God is Love

He who does not love does not know God; for God is love.
1 John 4:8

Webster defines love as an intense affectionate concern for another person or a passionate attraction to another person. Bartlett's *Familiar Quotations* has nearly one thousand quotations about love. Love defines us. How and how much we love is what others see in us and, more importantly, what God sees in us.

No man has ever seen God; if we love one another,
God abides in us and his love is perfected in us.
1 John 4:12

REFLECTION

HOW DO YOU DEFINE LOVE?
HOW DO YOU KNOW THAT GOD LOVES YOU?

July 10

God is Spirit

God is Spirit, and those who worship him
must worship in spirit and in truth.
John 4: 24

The paradox of spirit is that spirit is multi-dimensional and non-dimensional. Definitions of spirit include:

- the non-physical part of a person which is the seat of emotions
- the non-physical part of a person which survives physical death
- the prevailing quality, mood, or attitude of a person, group, or period of time

We are spirits in a human existence, not humans with a spiritual outlook. We find true peace when we fully trust that the Spirit controls our lives and we know that the Spirit works for good. With this joyous understanding, we demonstrate our faith.

Acquaint now thyself with him, and be at peace.
Job 22:21

REFLECTION

WHEN HAVE YOU FELT THE PRESENCE OF THE HOLY SPIRIT?
WHAT DID IT FEEL LIKE?

July 11

Ask, Seek, Knock

"And I tell you, Ask, and it will be given you; seek, and you will find;
knock, and it will be opened to you. For everyone who asks receives,
and he who seeks finds, and to him who knocks it will be opened."
Luke 11:9

If we ask for things from life, we are asking from a desire of self. Sometimes we ask for things we think we want, or should want, only to realize later that we did not want these things or the unintended consequences of having them. When we ask for things from God, seeking His will, and allow Him to be in control of the outcome, we get glorious results.

The more we think of ourselves, the less we are seeking God. Narrow the focus, seek God with your whole heart, concentrate on His presence.

Knocking on a closed door is taking action. It requires humility on our part. When we humble ourselves and take action, God opens the door to understanding.

Trust in the Lord with all your heart, and do not rely on
your own insight. In all your ways acknowledge him,
and he will make straight your paths.
Proverbs 3:5-6

REFLECTION

DO YOU REALLY THINK THAT GOD IS ALWAYS WITH YOU?
WHY OR WHY NOT?

July 12

Robust, Vigorous Confidence

Because you have kept my word of patient endurance,
I will keep you from the hour of trial...
Revelation 3:10

Trust yourself in God's hands.

Genuine faith is a robust, vigorous confidence, a total expectation that God is love, and God loves you. With true faith you abandon everything and have confidence in Him.

Powered by faith, life becomes a great adventure, with opportunities to find wonderful things in places we would never expect.

REFLECTION

WHAT MAKES YOU FEEL CLOSER TO GOD?

July 13

God Uses Us for His Purposes

...And who knows whether you have not come to the
kingdom for such a time as this?
Esther 4:14

The story of Esther is a beautiful demonstration. She was in a position as wife of the king to alter the future of her people. She had fears, doubts, and anxieties, but she was encouraged and guided by her cousin, Mordecai, a devout follower of God.

Our words and actions may be providing direction to those who look up to us. Do not allow discouragement or anxiety to interfere with this process.

REFLECTION

HOW DO YOU SEE THOSE AROUND YOU FAKING THEIR FAITH, TRUST,
AND STRENGTH? DO YOU EVER FIND YOURSELF DOING THIS?
IF YES, HOW CAN YOU COMBAT THIS?

July 14

Vision

Where there is no vision, the people cast off restraint... (ASV)
Proverbs 29:18

When we lose sight of God, we are drawn into reckless, sometimes risky behavior. Goals, ideals, and principles are great guidelines, but the vision must contain God. When our attitude is spiritually focused, and God is clearly in view, then we perform better, and we feel better for it. God can do greater things through us than we can anticipate.

Humble yourselves therefore under the mighty hand of God,
that in due time he may exalt you.
Cast all your anxieties on him, for he cares about you.
1 Peter 5:6-7

REFLECTION

HOW WOULD A COMPLETE, DEEPER TRUST IN GOD'S WORD
INFLUENCE YOUR READING OF THE BIBLE?

July 15
Redefine Success

...they left everything and followed him.
Luke 5:11

Are you on a path to success? Who defined that path? Are you really fulfilled by what you are doing and where you are going?

In Luke 5:10, James and John, sons of Zebedee, were partners with Simon (Peter) in a fishing business. The passage indicates that these three left their boats, homes, and families and followed Jesus when He called them to be fishermen of a different kind. They allowed God to define their path for them. They followed God's plan for them. There is no way they could have known what was to be the result of their efforts, they only knew that they were doing the right thing by following Jesus. These three ordinary fishermen were the first of twelve disciples Jesus called who enabled others to change their lives and follow Jesus. Their faith was part of a movement that changed the world.

*"There is no passion to be found in playing small, in settling
for a life that is less than the one you are capable of living."*
Nelson Mandela

REFLECTION

WHO ARE THE TRUE HEROES IN YOUR LIFE?
HOW DO YOU FEEL WHEN YOU THINK OF OR CONNECT WITH THEM?

July 16

Our Purpose

You did not choose me, but I chose you and appointed you that you should go and bear fruit and that your fruit should abide; so that whatever you ask the Father in my name, he may give it to you.
John 15:16

This is the call of God. Jesus is telling us that He chose us, we have a special purpose, and we are chosen by Him to accomplish this purpose. When we are answering God's call, He provides the means to accomplish our task. If we face our task as unhappy, dissatisfied, worried, or fearful, we are not following His will. We will remain unhappy, dissatisfied, worried, or fearful until we let our egos go and submit ourselves to accomplish what He means for us.

Complete harmony, happiness, and joy accompany His will for us. When we are in His will, they are as natural as the sunlight. When they are not present, it is time to seek them through prayer, meditation, and love.

REFLECTION

WHERE DO YOU NEED HEALING?

July 17

When God Speaks

*For the eyes of the Lord run to and fro throughout the whole earth,
to show his might in behalf of those
whose heart is perfect toward him.*
2 Chronicles 16:9

God speaks to us. When we hear Him, there should be no question of obedience. We may read a verse in the Bible one hundred times. The one hundred and first time we read it, the meaning is different, and we see truth that we did not see before. God is speaking to us, and our new perspective colors everything we see. This insight is the result of our obedience, a change in our own attitude, a new and deeper humbling of ourselves to His will.

REFLECTION

HOW DOES STUDYING THE WORD HELP YOU LIVE WITH COURAGE?

July 18
Kindness Is a Winning Attitude

A man who is kind benefits himself.
Proverbs 11:17

Showing kindness should always be our focus. Showing kindness may be difficult, and it even may seem undeserved at times. But showing kindness from internal motivation, with no script for the result, is rewarding in ways we cannot fully recognize. Acts of kindness can have a ripple effect or no immediate effect. In either case, it costs us nothing yet somewhere it pays dividends.

"When you have a choice between being right
and being kind, be kind."
Wayne Dyer

REFLECTION

WHY DO YOU THINK IT IS IMPORTANT
TO SEEK GOD'S DIRECTION WHEN MAKING DECISIONS?

July 19

When No One Is Looking

...whatever you do, do all to the glory of God.
1 Corinthians 10:31

We all face crises; we all have difficult times. It is one thing to go through the crisis in grand fashion, drawing attention to how we handle it. It is another thing entirely to go through every day glorifying God in everything we do when no one is paying attention. It is in these times and in this behavior that the power of God shows through. The aim is to manifest God's glory in our human lives, our human relationships, and our dealing with triumphs, disasters, and actual day-to-day conditions. Success is faithfulness in human life as it actually is.

...for God is at work in you, both to will
and to work for his good pleasure.
Philippians 2:13

REFLECTION

HOW DO YOU THINK GOD WANTS YOU TO APPLY
YOUR STRENGTHS, TALENTS, AND SKILLS WHERE YOU ARE TODAY?

July 20

Forgiveness and Consequences

*Do not be conformed to this world but be transformed by the renewal
of your mind, that you may prove what is the will of God,
what is good and acceptable and perfect.*
Romans 12:2

All of our sins are forgivable and all are forgiven by the grace
of God. This forgiveness is always available, only we must
make the choice to accept it. Cheap acceptance does not complete the fullness of God's grace. Consequences cannot be evaded
by a perfunctory prayer. Sincere repentance and complete acceptance of God's love provides the greatest reward that grace has to
offer. Finding grace has three essential parts:

- confess the sin and acknowledge its consequences
- forgive yourself because God has forgiven you
- change the behavior that caused you to sin

This is not an easy process, and it may require several attempts. Be faithful in your efforts to accomplish change so that
you may grow in your relationship with God.

*Almighty God, unto whom all hearts are open, all desires known, and
from whom no secrets are hid; cleanse the thoughts of our hearts by
the inspiration of thy Holy Spirit, that we may perfectly love Thee,
and worthily magnify thy Holy Name; through Christ our Lord.*
Holy Eucharist: Rite One, Episcopal Book of Common Prayer

REFLECTION

WHY DO YOU THINK CONFESSING YOUR SINS
IS NECESSARY FOR FORGIVENESS AND HEALING?

July 21

Get Up, Get Dressed, and Follow

And the angel said to him, "Dress yourself and put on your sandals."
And he did so. And he said to him, "Wrap your mantle
around you and follow me."
Acts 12:8

Peter's friend, James, had just been executed. Peter was in prison, and probably anticipated a similar outcome for himself. Then, in the middle of the night, the voice of an angel gave him specific instructions. He did what he was told to do and a miracle happened. Read Acts 12:8-17 for Peter's miraculous release from prison.

Get up, get dressed, and follow Christ. Don't worry about the obstacles. Don't let challenges of this world keep you from doing your best. God has sovereignty over all of it. Let go, let God do the work.

REFLECTION

WHAT MAKES YOU WANT TO SERVE GOD?

July 22

Conscience

So I always take pains to have a clear conscience
toward God and toward men.
Acts 24:16

Conscience is the inner expression of your highest values. When your thoughts and habits are God centered, when you strive to do what is good and acceptable to Him, your conscience will provide clear direction.

God's voice is often soft, gentle, and easy to miss, but it is there for us to listen to. God's word is always there for us. A deliberate act on our part is necessary to hear and heed this voice in order to "have a clear conscience toward God and toward men."

When you have an internal debate as to what to do—stop. Stop what you are doing and listen for direction from God.

REFLECTION

WHAT DO YOU NEED TO LET GO OF?

July 23
Using Talents Without Fear

...so I was afraid, and I went and hid your talent in the ground.
Matthew 25:25

Various phrases in the Bible command us not to fear. Phrases like "fear not," "have no fear," "do not be afraid" appear frequently in scripture. Depending on how the count is made, this command is found anywhere from 103 to 365 times. Whether it appears 365 times or 103 times is really irrelevant. At either count or anything in between, the command is there frequently so it must be an important part of having faith.

Fear is the basis of all negative thought. In the parable of the talents found in Matthew 25:14-30, Jesus explains the kingdom of heaven in the context of three servants who are given talents and how they are rewarded when it is time to settle accounts. The two servants who multiplied their talents were rewarded for their faithful obedience, while the servant who acted out of fear and did not use his talent was punished.

To be free of fear, we have to eliminate habits of fear-based thinking. When God gives us a task, we must step out and step up to accomplish His will. God will be with us.

REFLECTION

HOW HAS GOD RECENTLY MADE HIMSELF KNOWN IN YOUR LIFE?

July 24

Fear Not

Even though I walk through the valley of the shadow of death, I fear no evil; for thou art with me; thy rod and thy staff, they comfort me.
Psalm 23:4

Death itself has been conquered. By grace we are totally accepted just the way we are. God loves us. What is there to be afraid of? The ruler of the universe is our shepherd, our advocate, our protector, and our Savior.

Do not be anxious. In everything, by prayer and petition and with thanksgiving and expectation, present your requests to God.

Have no anxiety about anything, but in everything by prayer and supplication with thanksgiving let your requests be made known to God. And the peace of God, which passes all understanding, will keep your hearts and your minds in Christ Jesus.
Philippians 4:6-7

I lift up my eyes to the hills, from whence does my help come? My help comes from the Lord who made heaven and earth.
Psalm 121:1

The Lord is my light and my salvation; whom shall I fear? The Lord is the stronghold of my life, of whom shall I be afraid?
Psalm 27:1

God did not give us a spirit of timidity but a spirit of power
and love and self-control.
2 Timothy 1:7

...do not be anxious beforehand what you are to say; but say whatever
is given you in that hour, for it is not you who speak,
but the Holy Spirit.
Mark 13:11

Cast all your anxieties on him, for he cares about you.
1 Peter 5:7

REFLECTION

WHAT CONTEMPORARY METAPHOR WOULD YOU USE
TO ILLUSTRATE THE SHEPHERD'S PROTECTION?

July 25

Be Strong and of Good Courage

…Be strong and of good courage; be not frightened, neither be dismayed; for the LORD your God is with you wherever you go.
Joshua 1:9

Courage is not learned from instruction. We gain courage as a result of encountering danger, real or imagined, and overcoming it.

We gain strength and self-confidence every time we face fear and work through it.

"… as I was with Moses, so I will be with you;
I will not fail you or forsake you."
Joshua 1:5

REFLECTION

WHAT DO YOU FEEL LIKE YOU NEED TO PROVE AND TO WHOM?

July 26
Love Bears All Things

*So we know and believe the love God has for us. God is love, and
he who abides in love abides in God, and God in him. In this is
love perfected with us, that we may have confidence for the day of
judgment, because as he is so are we in this world.*
1 John 4:16-17

God's love is an active, assertive, and positive emotion that reflects our confidence in God's presence in our lives. In love,
we bear the unbearable, believe what seems to be unbelievable, and
hope when all seems hopeless.

*Love bears all things, believes all things,
hopes all things, endures all things.*
1 Corinthians 13:7

REFLECTION

NAME THREE WAYS LOVE IS IMPORTANT IN YOUR LIFE?

July 27
Teach Me the Way

Let me hear in the morning of thy steadfast love,
for in thee I put my trust.
Teach me the way I should go, for to thee I lift up my soul.
Psalm 143:8

Amid the daily noise, God is speaking to us constantly. It is up to us to get away from distractions and open our hearts and minds to His soft, tender, yet strong voice. The voice is there providing direction. The reward for listening and heeding His word may not be readily apparent, but it is there nonetheless.

Stop, listen, learn, and follow with love and courage.

"Quiet yourself before God for a season and ask
him to make you newly aware of his love for you.
Let him use whatever instrument he chooses."
Charles Stanley

For thus says the high and lofty One who inhabits eternity,
whose name is Holy:
"I dwell in the high and holy place, and also with him who is of a
contrite and humble spirit, to revive the spirit of the humble, and to
revive the heart of the contrite..."
Isaiah 57:15

REFLECTION

WHAT HABITS, ACTIVITIES, OR ATTITUDES
DO YOU NEED TO CHANGE? WHY?

July 28
Satan's Last Stand

For he who finds me finds life and obtains favor from the Lord.
Proverbs 8:35

Satan's last stand is negative thought. When you have managed to remove evil, doubt, and fear from every other facet of your life, his last approach is negative analysis. "There is no way..." "You prayed before and look what happened..." "You really don't deserve..."— and so on, and so on, and so on. These thoughts are placed there to derail you. This is the time to quietly know the Truth and hold on to it tightly.

It is not when things are going well that we progress. When things are going wrong and we find refuge in prayer, we can move forward. When we are faced with discouragement and despair due to negative analysis, and we stand firm in our faith, we make major strides in our knowledge of the Truth.

REFLECTION

WHAT NEGATIVE THOUGHTS DO YOU HAVE ABOUT YOUR LIFE'S
PURPOSE, YOUR FRIENDS, YOUR CURRENT CIRCUMSTANCES?
MAKE A LIST AND IDENTIFY STRATEGIES.
HOW WILL YOU DEAL WITH THEM?

July 29

With All Your Heart

Trust in the Lord with all your heart,
and do not rely on your own insight.
Proverbs 3:5

God's plan for us exceeds anything we could plan in life. When we take our eyes off of God and look only to our own circumstances, we cannot see the things He has in store for us.

Read 1 Samuel 17 and consider the shepherd. David was a young boy who worked as a shepherd watching sheep that move slowly eating grass, drinking water, and sleeping. Not an exciting job for a bright, active, young boy. It should not be surprising to learn that David practiced with his sling for hours on end using leaves on the trees as targets and challenging himself with ever increasing distances. His work also involved rescuing sheep from predators.

From these humble tasks, David learned skills that prepared him for greater works in God's plan for him. Slinging a rock to hit a small, unarmored area of the giant Goliath's forehead would not be difficult for a young boy who had the skill David developed in his daily work.

Even more important, David was impassioned by his love of God.

Then David said to the Philistine, "You come to me with a sword and a spear and with a javelin; but I come to you in the name of the Lord of hosts, the God of the armies of Israel, whom you have defied."
1 Samuel 17:45

When David accepted his role of shepherd, he gained the experience to enhance his skills as a hunter and protector of his flock. He did not know God's plan for him, but he made good use of his circumstances without realizing he was being prepared for his first major role in God's plan.

Keep sound wisdom and discretion...and they will be life for your soul and adornment for your neck.
Proverbs 3:21

...for the Lord will be your confidence...
Proverbs 3:26

REFLECTION

LIST SEVERAL EXAMPLES OF WHAT YOU CONSIDER SACRIFICIAL LOVE?

July 30

Why?

... the LORD gave, and the LORD has taken away;
blessed be the name of the LORD.
Job 1:21

Job has lost everything. He had nothing left but his faith, and he demonstrated his faith by accepting his situation and blessing the name of the Lord. As he observes, God is greater than all of the adversity, all of the pain, and all of the challenges of this world.

When these situations occur, it is natural for us as humans to ask "why." Sometimes we learn why, sometimes we don't. In either case, these situations offer us an opportunity to learn and grow spiritually.

The story of Job demonstrates God's involvement in our lives. When we release our defiance and disbelief, God's presence can become more profound. Our defiance and disbelief only limit the extent to which God becomes involved in our lives.

Job not only accepts his fate with faith, he prays for his friends. God answers his prayer and forgives his friends for their lack of faith. He then restores the fortunes of Job by giving him twice as much as he had before.

And the Lord restored the fortunes of Job, when he had prayed for his
friends; and the Lord gave Job twice as much as he had before.
Job 42: 10

REFLECTION

WHAT CONVINCES YOU OF GOD'S LOVE FOR YOU?

July 31

The Responsibility of Dominion

When I look at the heavens, the work of thy fingers...
Thou hast given him dominion over the works of thy hands;
thou hast put all things under his feet. ...
O Lord, our Lord, how majestic is thy name in all the earth.
Psalm 8:3,6, 9

This psalm contemplates the majesty and splendor of God's creation as well as the royal gift we are given in the midst of it all.

How insignificant we are, yet we have been blessed with the responsibility of stewardship of His wonderful creation. Do not take the blessing or the responsibility lightly. Every plant, every animal, every drop of sunlight is filled with blessing and hope. We are to love, honor, and appreciate the bounty in all of these and share our appreciation with others.

When we truly grasp the abundance of His supply, we can trust that He will provide for every real need we have.

And my God will supply every need of yours
according to his riches in glory in Jesus Christ.
Philippians 4:19

REFLECTION

HOW DOES GOD CALL OUT TO YOU
THROUGH THE BEAUTY OF THIS WORLD?

August 1

Awe and Gratitude

A glad heart makes a cheerful countenance...
Proverbs 15:13

Our environment is pretty much what we make it. When we allow the negativity of the world to shape our attitude, we pursue a self-perpetuating downward spiral.

When we look with awe and gratitude at the wonderful positive things that surround us, it is quickly reflected in our appearance as well as our behavior.

...a cheerful heart has a continual feast.
Proverbs 15:15

REFLECTION

LIST WHAT YOU CONSIDER YOUR TOP THREE BLESSINGS TODAY.
HOW DO THESE MAKE YOU FEEL? WHY THESE THREE?

August 2

Mind Your Own Business

When Peter saw him, he said to Jesus, "Lord, what about this man?"
Jesus said to him "If it is my will that he remain until I come,
what is that to you? Follow me!"
John 21:21-22

One of the more difficult lessons we must learn is to mind our own business when it comes to interfering with God's plan for others. What He chooses to give to others or make from them is His business. We should be thankful for and appreciate what He has chosen to give us.

We have enough to deal with in keeping ourselves on His path and confronting the matters of this world. Energy spent in judging or correcting others is wasted. It can be better utilized in contributing to our personal behavior and spiritual growth.

REFLECTION

HOW HAS SOMEONE ELSE AFFECTED YOU IN A NEGATIVE WAY?
HOW DID YOU DEAL WITH IT?

August 3

Teach Me

Teach me the way I should go, for to thee I lift up my soul.
Psalm143:8b

We are constantly being instructed in the way we should go. However, we are not constantly listening to God's instruction.

God's plan for us leads us to peace and prosperity in His kingdom. When we drop our agenda and listen for God's voice, our perspective and our conditions change. If the conditions are unpleasant, there is something to learn. If the conditions are pleasant, there is something to learn. All experiences are to prepare us for what is to come—peace and prosperity in His kingdom.

Teach me to do thy will, for thou art my God!
Psalm 143:10

REFLECTION

HOW WILL YOU ENCOURAGE OTHERS TODAY?

August 4

Let Us Not Grow Weary

… in order that God's purpose of election might continue,
not because of works but because of his call.
Romans 9:11

When we align our purpose with God's purpose for us, we find strength and courage. Unfortunately, we often choose the site of our own martyrdom when we disclaim God's purpose or use our talents in a manner not intended by God.

If your lot is sweet, enjoy and learn. If your lot is bitter, seek the lesson and grow. In either case, it is only temporary. Look for God's presence in all conditions and trust Him.

We know that in everything God works for good with those who love
him, who are called according to his purpose.
Romans 8:28

REFLECTION

WHAT MAKES YOU WEARY? HOW DO YOU HANDLE THAT?

August 5

Work It Out

*I pray that the eyes of your heart may be enlightened in order that you
may know the hope to which he has called you,
the riches of his glorious inheritance in his holy people...* (NIV)
Ephesians 1:18

We must work through what God has placed in our paths. We
cannot do anything to earn salvation, but we are called to
manifest it in order that others may also receive it.

We are here to be channels of God's work. When we completely submit to His will, we are allowing His work to be done
through us. The challenges we encounter are there for a reason.
Sometimes God is only providing them in order to deliver the message to us that we can overcome them.

*...he has granted to us his precious and very great promises, that
through these you may escape from the corruption that is in the world
because of passion and become partakers of the divine nature.*
1 Peter 1:4

REFLECTION

WHY DO YOU THINK WE HAVE DIFFICULTY
ADMITTING TO SIN AND ERRORS?

August 6

Significance

Now when they saw the boldness of Peter and John, and perceived that they were uneducated, common men, they wondered; and they recognized that they had been with Jesus.

Acts 4:13

Significance is not defined by worldly accomplishments. Titles, degrees, and social positions are not true measures of our success. Fame and fortune in this world do not assure position in the Kingdom. All of these things are temporary. Here today, gone tomorrow, and completely forgotten in the future.

True significance is the impact God provides through our faith, witness, and demonstration. This cannot be accomplished without abandoning our worship of worldly things and being connected with God. Our relationship with God is eternal, substantial, and significant. God works through us. The significance He provides through us impacts lives in an eternal way, an impact that titles, degrees, and social positions never could.

REFLECTION

WHEN, WHERE, AND WHY HAVE YOU BEEN A VICTIM OF PRIDE?

The Top Five Regrets

Brothers, I do not consider that I have made it my own.
But one thing I do: forgetting what lies behind and straining forward
to what lies ahead, I press on toward the goal for the prize
of the upward call of God in Christ Jesus.
Philippians 3:13

Research has revealed that the top five regrets of the dying include (not in any particular order):

- not living a life true to themselves but instead living according to the expectations of others.
- working too hard.
- not having courage to express their true feelings.
- losing track of friends.
- not letting themselves be happier.

When we endeavor daily to walk the path God has for us and make use of the gifts and talents God has given us in the best manner we can, we will be living in way that avoids these regrets.

REFLECTION

WHAT DO YOU REGRET NOW THAT YOU CAN FIX?

August 8

Repentance and Change

For godly grief produces a repentance that leads
to salvation and brings no regret.
2 Corinthians 7:10

Guilt and regret distract us from our true purpose. Repent and change, but do not dwell on guilt and regret. Do not spend any time trying to change the past. It will not happen. Instead, focus on the changes to make and the things to make happen in the future.

Yes, we can learn from past mistakes, and we can thank God for those disappointments and failures that lead us to acknowledge our dependence on Him. However, we must focus on the talents we have been blessed with and the successes God has provided. We can then seek to serve Him with renewed energy and confidence.

For as the heavens are high above the earth, so great is his steadfast
love for those who fear him; as far as the east is from the west,
so far does he remove our transgressions from us.
Psalm 103:11-12

REFLECTION

WHAT DOES REPENTANCE FEEL LIKE TO YOU?

August 9
Facing Life's Challenges

"I came that they may have life and have it abundantly."
John 10:10

Even as believers, we experience periods of despair, and when we are going through them, our outcome is unclear. Every now and then, there are miraculous rescues. Regardless, both the challenge and the outcome, whatever they may be, help us grow in our faith. God asks us to continue to trust Him even when we don't understand His plan.

In the midst of the challenge, the quickest way to get our mind off of ourselves and put it on God's power is to praise Him, knowing that His plan for us is life, abundant life. Praising God in times of difficulty shows defiance to fear, anxiety, and doubt. This is not a logical response, but it is an effective one!

The Lord is merciful and gracious, slow to anger
and abounding in steadfast love.
Psalm 103:8

REFLECTION

WHAT IS YOUR DEEPEST HURT?

August 10

Let Go, Let God

Many are the plans in the mind of a man,
but it is the purpose of the Lord that will be established.
Proverbs 19:21

We are the channels through which God's plan is realized. The first step for us is to get out of our own way.

When we think of our own limitations and all of the reasons why peace, harmony, and joy are not possible in a given set of circumstances, we are shutting out God. This is a lesson we must relearn frequently. Stop thinking about the difficulty or problem and think about God with prayer and thanksgiving. Thank God for being with you during the difficulty and for helping you understand what it is teaching you. Thank God for your blessings as well. Then get out of the way and let God do the work.

But Jesus looked at them and said to them, "With men this is
impossible, but with God all things are possible."
Matthew 19:26

REFLECTION

HOW DO YOU MANAGE CIRCUMSTANCES DURING TIMES OF DOUBT?

August 11
Making Right Decisions

Agree with God, and be at peace; thereby good will come to you.
Job 22:21

When you encounter a situation where you have to make a difficult decision, be encouraged by the fact that this decision contains blessings for you and all concerned. Seek wisdom and direction through prayer and mentally surround the decision and all who are involved in love—complete, total, and unconditional love. Then wait in open expectation for an answer.

The fear of the Lord is the beginning of wisdom,
and the knowledge of the Holy One is insight.
Proverbs 9:10

A man's mind plans his way, but the Lord directs his steps.
Proverbs 16:9

REFLECTION

WHY DO YOU THINK GOD ALLOWS US TO DO HIS WORK?

August 12
The Reward of Personal Discipline

For the moment all discipline seems painful rather than pleasant;
later it yields the peaceful fruit of righteousness
to those who have been trained by it.
Hebrews 12:11

When we are ready to pursue God's plan, we will find that everything else is ready too.

Therefore lift your drooping hands and strengthen your weak knees,
and make straight the paths for your feet...
Hebrews 12: 12-13

Be not wise in your own eyes, fear the Lord and turn away from evil.
Proverbs 3:7

He who pursues righteousness and kindness will find life and honor.
Proverbs 21:21

REFLECTION

WHAT ARE YOU AVOIDING TODAY
THAT YOU KNOW GOD WANTS YOU TO DO?

August 13

We Must Prepare

*Always be prepared to make a defense against anyone who calls you to
account for the hope that is in you, yet do it with gentleness
and reverence; and keep your conscience clear...*
1 Peter 3:15-16

We are to be in the world, but not of it. We must face
those things which interfere with our spiritual energy—
temptations of all sorts, fear, and disappointments—yet defend
ourselves with gentleness and reverence.

We do not need to be afraid, but we do need to be prepared,
not just for ourselves but also for those who may be transformed
by witnessing our peace.

*...whatever is true, whatever is honorable, whatever is just, whatever
is pure, whatever is lovely, whatever is gracious, if there is any
excellence, if there is anything worthy of praise, think about these
things. What you have learned and received and heard and seen in
me, do; and the God of peace will be with you.*
Philippians 4:8-9

*My fruit is better than gold, even fine gold,
and my yield better than choice silver.*
Proverbs 8:19

REFLECTION

WHAT CAN YOU DO TODAY
TO DEMONSTRATE YOUR LOVE FOR OTHERS?

August 14

Renewal and Transformation

*Put off your old nature which belongs to your former manner of life
and is corrupt through deceitful lusts, and be renewed in the Spirit of
your minds, and put on the new nature, created after the likeness of
God in true righteousness and holiness.*
Ephesians 4:22-24

Everything else falls into place when we realize that our greatest good is our service to God. When we trust God's perfect planning and accept His perfect timing, our lives take on a new meaning. Those things we thought we could not do without often become meaningless shackles. The people we attract into our lives are different, things we want to do change, and the world takes on a bright, glorious hue.

*Do not be conformed to this world, but be transformed by the
renewing of your mind, so that you may discern what is the good,
pleasing, and perfect will of God.*
Romans 12:2

REFLECTION

IN WHAT WAYS ARE YOU TRYING TO LIVE A CHRIST-LIKE LIFE?
WHAT CHANGES HAVE YOU MADE?

August 15

We Are Prisoners of False Beliefs

Bring me out of prison, that I may give thanks to thy name! The
righteous will surround me; for thou wilt deal bountifully with me.
Psalm 142:7

There is a legend about a citizen who was arrested and placed
in a dungeon. The huge door of his cell was shut with a loud
clang, and he remained in that dark, damp cell for many years. Each
day the big door would open with a loud creaking noise, his daily
allotment of bread and water would be thrust in by a fierce looking
jailer, and the door would close again.

Finally, the prisoner decided he preferred death to continued
existence in this situation, but he did not want to commit sui-
cide. He imagined a plot whereby he would attack the fierce jailer
the next day and be killed by him. In preparation, he decided to
examine the door. He took the huge handle in his hand and discovered that the door was not locked. He turned the handle, and
the door opened because there was no lock. He crawled along the
dark corridor and felt his way up the stairs. At the top of the stairs,
several soldiers were talking, but they made no attempt to stop
him. He crossed the yard, passed the armed guard who paid no
attention to him, and walked out of the prison. For all those years,
he had been a captive, a captive of false belief.

We are all prisoners of some false belief. If nothing else, we are
prisoners of our own reluctance to forgive ourselves. We wallow in
guilt and self-criticism when the truth is we have already been forgiven and accepted. Accept the fact that you are totally accepted!

REFLECTION

WHAT AREAS OF YOUR LIFE DO YOU NEED GOD
TO ENABLE YOU TO BE PURER?

August 16

The Vine and the Branches

"I am the vine, you are the branches. He who abides in me,
and I in him, he it is that bears much fruit,
for apart from me you can do nothing."
John 15:5

In these words, Jesus explains the true source of all things. When we have faith in God—abide in Him and allow Him dominion in our lives—we bear His fruit in abundance.

In business, in human relationships, in personal finances, in all things we encounter, if we make God our partner and include Him in every facet of our lives, the results can be amazing. The fruit we bear in those areas will be a blessing to us and to all who are exposed to it. We will partake of His fruit—peace, joy, and happiness—in all areas of our lives.

In all your ways acknowledge him, and he will direct your paths.
Proverbs 3:6

REFLECTION

**HOW CAN YOU WITNESS THIS WEEK
IN THE AREAS THAT SEEM ORDINARY?**

August 17
The Vinedresser

"I am the true vine, and my Father is the Vinedresser. Every branch of mine that bears no fruit, he takes away, and every branch that does bear fruit he prunes, that it may bear more fruit."
John 15:1-3

Our thoughts produce our actions, our actions produce fruit. It is important that we purposefully direct our thoughts to positive action, that we think of and appreciate the abundance that is in everything we see.

Our purpose in God's plan is to bear fruit. The type of fruit is determined by the talents, preferences, and passions He has given us. The pruning we go through may be painful, but He provides the pruning in order that we may bear more fruit.

But the fruit of the Spirit is love, joy, peace, patience, kindness, goodness, faithfulness, gentleness, self-control...
Galatians 5:22-23

REFLECTION

WHO WAS YOUR FAVORITE TEACHER? WHY?
WHAT DID YOU LEARN FROM HIM/HER?

August 18

The Seven Habits of Joy

The only true measure of personal success is joy. The highest expression of joy is making other people happy. It's nearly impossible to make others happy if you do not have joy.

Here are seven habits that can be accomplished with small changes in your daily routine. If you are like most people, adopting these habits will increase the joy in your life:

1. Begin with grateful anticipation.

Before you rise in the morning, while still in bed and waking up, make your first thoughts: "Thank you, God, for this beautiful day and all the blessings it contains!" Think to yourself that something wonderful is going to happen today!

2. Take time to plan, prioritize, and reflect.

Most stress comes from the perception that you have too much to do. Rather than stress about it, pick one thing that will move you closer to your highest goal and purpose in life. Make your mission for the day to do that first.

3. Give a small gift to everyone you meet.

Your gift can be your smile, a word of encouragement, a gesture of politeness, a thank you, or even a friendly hello. You may be a light of that person's day.

4. Assume all other people have good intentions.

You really don't know what is making people do what they do. Assuming that they have bad intentions only adds misery to your life, while assuming good intentions adds mystery, excitement, and joy.

5. Eat good food and savor every bite.

When you take time for a meal, even a quick meal, eat good food, be thankful for it, focus on it, and savor it.

6. Let go of things you cannot control.

We create anxiety when we focus on circumstances or events that we do not and cannot control. Focus on the task at hand and give it your best effort, then let it go.

7. End with thanksgiving just as you began with thanksgiving.

Just before you go to bed, reflect on your day and write down at least one wonderful thing that happened. It might be a smile from someone or an unexpected outcome from an unpleasant circumstance. Be grateful for all that God has given you that day.

REFLECTION

HOW CAN YOU ADD MORE JOY TO YOUR DAYS
WITH THESE SEVEN HABITS?

August 19

Perfect Peace

Thou dost keep him in perfect peace, whose mind is stayed on thee, because he trusts in thee.
Isaiah 26:3

Peace is not lack of conflict nor is it a state of personal bliss. God's peace is not about our circumstances. It's about being aligned with His will. Our circumstances are opportunities to glorify God.

There is nothing wrong with wanting stability and prosperity in our lives. There is nothing sinful about seeking ways to eliminate conflict and "make peace" with our neighbors. However, these things do not take the place of inner peace.

Paul's life was full of things we do not typically associate with peace: imprisonment, shipwrecks, and beatings (see 2 Corinthians 11:23-28), but he had an inner peace that carried him through these things and enabled him to accomplish great things in glorifying God. As we strive to meet God's will, we will find a refuge in Him and a kind of peace only He can provide.

Rejoice in the Lord always; again I will say, Rejoice. Let all men know your forbearance. The Lord is at hand. Have no anxiety about anything, but in everything by prayer and supplication with thanksgiving let your requests be made known to God. And the peace of God, which passes all understanding, will keep your hearts and your minds in Christ Jesus.
Philippians 4: 4-7

REFLECTION

WHAT KEEPS YOU FROM HAVING INNER PEACE?
HOW CAN YOU CHANGE THAT?

August 20

We Receive What We Give

Do not be conformed to this world but be transformed by the renewal of your mind, that you may prove what is the will of God, what is good and acceptable and perfect.
Romans 12:2

We respond to the conditions of our lives with the thoughts we have about them. The paradox of this is that our external conditions are often the expression of our inner thoughts. If you treat every phase of your life with positive thoughts and loving attitudes, you will be amazed at the outcome that returns to you.

But be doers of the word, not hearers only, deceiving yourselves.
James 1:22

REFLECTION

HOW HAVE YOU EXPERIENCED
YOUR POSITIVE ATTITUDE AFFECTING SOMEONE'S SPIRIT?

August 21

Faith and Works

For as the body apart from the spirit is dead,
so faith apart from works is dead.
James 2:26

Others not only see what we do but also how we respond to our circumstances, and our actions are impressed on them, either positively or negatively, by what they see. Our lives are an expression of our attitudes. As we grow in faith, as we move further along on our faith journey, our outer lives should reflect the same growth, reflecting positive wellbeing in our deepening relationship with God. We must always remember, whether our actions and works are positive and uplifting or negative and defeating, they generate results in the world and impact those around us. Walking in faith is sometimes hard work, but the results are real and measurable.

We love, because he first loved us.
1 John 4:19

Beloved, let us love one another; for love is of God,
and he who loves is born of God and knows God.
1 John 4: 7

REFLECTION

HOW CAN YOU BE A POSITIVE ROLE MODEL?

August 22

Our Gifts

Now there are varieties of gifts, but the same Spirit...
1 Corinthians 12:4

Have you ever considered what life would be like if we were all the same? What if everyone had the same gifts or talents? Our world would be less interesting! The variety of gifts we have received makes life collaborative, innovative, rich, and full of different views of "reality."

All of us have access to the same Spirit. That Spirit impacts our reality as we allow it to. The more we emphasize the Spirit in our lives, the more our lives reflect His glory. The quality of our lives is dependent upon how we utilize our gifts to glorify the Spirit.

...whatever you do, do all to the glory of God.
1 Corinthians 10:31

REFLECTION

HOW DO YOU THINK OTHERS VIEW YOU AT WORK?
IN SOCIAL CIRCLES?

August 23

Fresh Starts

*...forgetting what lies behind and straining forward to what lies
ahead, I press on toward the goal for the prize
of the upward call of God...*
Philippians 3:13-14

The Bible tells us over and over that God is a God of fresh starts. There are promises of grace, forgiveness, new beginnings, and seemingly impossible dreams coming true. Let the past remain in the past and look forward and upward faithfully, trusting in God's healing and generous provision.

*...Remember not the former things, nor consider the things of old.
Behold, I am doing a new thing; now it springs forth...*
Isaiah 43: 18-19

REFLECTION

ISAIAH SAYS GOD IS DOING A NEW THING IN THE SCRIPTURE ABOVE.

WHAT DOES THAT MEAN TO YOU?

August 24

The Power Within You

Trust in the Lord with all your heart,
and do not rely on your own insight.
Proverbs 3:5

When we allow God to take over, He will direct all of our affairs. We are handing over these responsibilities to the all-powerful, all-knowing, and tireless One who will joyfully carry them.

Cast your burden on the Lord, and he will sustain you.
Psalm 55:22

REFLECTION

WHAT AREAS OF YOUR LIFE NEED "RECKLESS ABANDON" TO GOD?

August 25

Forgiveness Begins with Forgiving Yourself

I will arise and go to my father, and I will say to him, "Father, I have sinned against heaven and before you; I am no longer worthy to be called your son; treat me as one of your hired servants."
Luke 15:18-19

The parable of the prodigal son in Luke 15:11-32 tells us about a young man who had really made a mess of his life. He was sure that he was no longer worthy of his father's love and that he was not worthy to be called his father's son, but he found that his father loved him anyway.

We are a lot like him when we believe we are unworthy of love. Like the father in this parable, God's love is always there. God's love for us is total, complete, and unconditional. Because we are human and make mistakes, we create circumstances that make us feel unworthy. When we see ourselves as God sees us, the negative things we believe about ourselves fade, and we open ourselves to receive His unconditional love.

The Lord, your God, is in your midst, a warrior who gives victory; he will rejoice over you with gladness, he will renew you in his love...
Zephaniah 3:17

REFLECTION

WHAT BURDENS, PAINFUL MEMORIES, OR DARK SECRETS
DO YOU NEED TO CARRY TO GOD?

August 26
The Danger of Anger

...first be reconciled with your brother,
and then come and offer your gift.
Matthew 5:24

Resentment, revenge, indignation, and all other forms of anger get in the way of spiritual power.

Whoever is angry with another is in danger of missing the benefits of having that person's friendship as well as the lessons to be learned from that relationship. We are all either teachers or students, depending upon the time and circumstances. Anger prevents either role from being fully realized, and both parties miss out.

REFLECTION

WHAT MAKES YOU ANGRY? HOW DO YOU MANAGE YOUR ANGER?

August 27
A Basic Psychological Truth

Apply your mind to instruction and your ear to words of knowledge...
Proverbs 23:12

We are controlled by what we think and what we think about. This is a basic psychological truth. There is substantial evidence that thought can have physical manifestation in our bodies as well as in our minds.

This is good news if our thoughts are about good, healthful, helpful, and beautiful things. Often, we manifest more physical wellbeing. Unfortunately, when we focus on fear, jealousy, vengeance, anger, disappointment, or any negative condition, we allow space for them to grow...and they will. Root them out and replace them with good thoughts instead.

REFLECTION

HOW HAS GOD BEEN TEACHING YOU ABOUT LOVE RECENTLY?

August 28
Dance Like No One Is Watching

*And David and all the house of Israel were making merry before the L*ORD *with all their might, with songs and lyres and harps and tambourines and castanets and cymbals.*
2 Samuel 6:5

King David and the people of Israel had defeated the Philistines and recaptured the Ark of the Covenant, which represented the presence of God. David and the people were filled with joy, so filled that they made music and danced. This was no ordinary dance. It was a dance of uninhibited, unrestrained praise to the Lord in response to His presence and His victory.

God is present with us every day. Yet, we miss so many opportunities to celebrate His presence with joy. We sometimes respond with reverence, and that is good. However, there are times when we should show our faith and gratitude with open, uninhibited celebration.

REFLECTION

IS TODAY SUCH A TIME? DANCE LIKE NO ONE IS WATCHING!

August 29

The Purpose of Our Salvation

In all toil there is profit, but mere talk tends only to want.
Proverbs 14:23

God offered Jesus as a sacrifice in order that everyone through Him might be saved. The purpose of this extremely generous act and the gift of grace is not that we may be saved from hell, but that we may manifest the life of Jesus in our own lives.

Keep yourself fit to let the life of Jesus be manifested in you. Your circumstances are the means of manifesting. We exhibit His life most noticeably when we respond to life with "what would Jesus do?"

You cannot keep yourself fit by exercising self-pity, resentment, anxiety, or selfishness. Fitness results from regular exercise of prayer, meditation, praise, and thanksgiving.

REFLECTION

**HOW WILL YOU LET THE WORD OF GOD
BE LIVING AND ACTIVE IN YOU?**

August 30

Consider the Lilies

"Consider the lilies of the field, how they grow;
they neither toil nor spin..."
Matthew 6:28

We provide the most effective lives when we live simply and unaffectedly, providing examples to others and exhibiting our dependence on God.

We are where we are, in the condition we are in, regardless of our willingness to accept our position and those conditions. Our relationship with God remains in place, and it is up to us to find ways to improve this relationship by accepting outer conditions and trusting God to show us ways to change. This change may be within ourselves, the conditions themselves, or in our perspective toward these conditions. We may be surprised to discover the blessings they contain and the beautiful new world we find when we accept and follow God's guidance. There are times when God's love defies human logic.

Who shall separate us from the love of Christ? Shall tribulation,
or distress, or persecution, or famine, or nakedness, or peril, or
sword?... No, in all these things we are more
than conquerors through him who loved us.
Romans 8:35, 37

REFLECTION

WHAT AREAS OF YOUR LIFE ARE CURRENTLY
CAUSING THE MOST WORRY OR ANXIETY?
WHAT WOULD YOU TRUST GOD TO DO WITH THESE AREAS?

August 31

We Are One

"...that they all may be one..."
John 17:21

This is part of Christ's prayer after His resurrection. He is praying in the presence of His disciples following His explanation of what is about to happen to Him. "I am leaving the world and going to the Father" (John 16:28).

Jesus is praying for His disciples prior to His ascension. His prayer is that they may realize and represent to the world that they are part of One Body. This unity will provide strength and courage as they proceed into the world to accomplish His mission.

This is His prayer for all of His followers. His desire, His request, and our purpose is that we accept our position as part of One Body and demonstrate our belief to the world in order that others may realize their positions as part of this One Body.

"...even as We are one"
John 17:22

REFLECTION

WHAT DOES IT MEAN TO YOU TO BE PART OF THE ONE BODY?

September 1
First Things First

For we are the temple of the living God; as God said,
"I will live in them and move among them,
and I will be their God, and they shall be my people."
2 Corinthians 6:16

When we put God first, our perspective on the matters of this world is altered—not diminished, but altered. We see things in a different light because of the Light.

When we contribute to God's work, and by our efforts show that we are putting God first, our lives will never be the same. When we don't make ourselves part of the plan, God's work will still get done, God's name will still be glorified, only we will miss being part of that experience. We will miss the rewards that God wants to pour into our lives.

Since we have these promises, beloved, let us cleanse
ourselves from every defilement of body and spirit,
and make holiness perfect in the fear of God.
2 Corinthians 7:1

REFLECTION

YOUR BODY IS GOD'S TEMPLE. WHAT DOES THAT MEAN TO YOU?

September 2

Help My Unbelief

Immediately the father of the child cried out and said,
"I believe; help my unbelief!"
Mark 9:24

Even the most faithful among us tend to spend time with one foot in the valley of unbelief while the other is ready to climb the mountain of belief. In this passage, as in many others, Jesus does not require the father to believe completely before healing his child. Jesus met him where he was in his belief.

He will meet any of us wherever we are in our walk of faith too. It is up to us to call upon Him and believe that He will answer.

And Jesus said to him… "All things are possible to him who believes."
Mark 9:23

REFLECTION

WHAT DOUBTS DO YOU WANT TO SHARE WITH GOD?

September 3
Pray Without Ceasing

...pray continually, give thanks in all circumstances; for this is God's
will for you in Christ Jesus.
1 Thessalonians 5:17-18

Prayer is a way of life. Our prayer practice is most effective when we consider it as simple and necessary as breathing.

God answers prayers. The answer is not always what we expected, but there is an answer. Jesus expressed certainty that prayer is always answered. When we humble ourselves as He did and accept the answers as He did, we are more likely to see the answers. Unfortunately, we often preconceive the answer in human, worldly terms, which often results in disappointment.

Consider the answer in supernatural terms. The picture is much bigger than we can possibly understand. The answer is always for what is best.

...in everything God works for good with those who love him.
Romans 8:28

REFLECTION

HOW CAN YOU SUBMIT YOUR DECISIONS AT WORK TO GOD?

September 4

Choose to Rejoice!

Rejoice in the Lord always, again I will say, Rejoice!
Philippians 4:4

Paul is addressing the Christians at Philippi while he is in prison. This was his first church in Europe, and his relationship with them was warm. His outlook in the letter was that what has happened to him served to advance the gospel.

God's plan is often obscured by human emotion, but it is always for our ultimate best interests. When we are undergoing trials, rejoicing may not seem to be our first choice of emotion, but where we can rejoice, like Paul, is that even in trials God is with us.

REFLECTION

NAME TWO OF YOUR GREATEST FEARS.
HOW DO YOU FEEL GOD IS PRESENT WITH YOU THROUGH THEM?

September 5

Pursue Diligently

He who pursues righteousness and faithful love will find love,
righteousness and honor.
Proverbs 21:21

I have chosen the way of faithfulness, I set thy ordinances before me.
Psalm 119:30

Webster defines diligence as the persistent, attentive, and energetic application to a task. Benjamin Franklin said that diligence was the mother of luck. Faithful work toward a goal often brings good results. Your future depends largely upon your current mental conduct and the actions you take. Be active in pursuing your faith. Understand what God requires from His people and make those your "ordinances" to honor and follow. Remember to love God and love His children.

Do not be conformed to this world, but be transformed by the renewal
of your mind, that you may prove what is the will of God,
what is good and acceptable and perfect.
Romans 12:2

REFLECTION

WHAT IS YOUR ATTITUDE TOWARD DISCIPLINE?

September 6

Whom Do You Serve?

"No one can serve two masters..."
Matthew 7:24

We are spirits in human bodies. We grow best when we serve our spiritual master. When we try to do everything ourselves by serving a material, worldly master, we must face the consequences of materialism. One consequence is that we never have enough of whatever it is to satisfy us. In setting material goals, our focus is usually on the gap between what we have and what we want. When we focus on the distance between what we have and what we want that distance tends to grow.

In spiritual matters, it is very difficult to see any distance ahead, to know what tomorrow holds. We simply must have faith and be prepared to do God's work as it comes to us. That is the path to satisfaction—serving the master who offers us love and eternal life.

This acceptance, combined with a desire to grow spiritually, generates true spiritual growth. With this in mind, when we look back after a period of time, we can see how we have grown spiritually, and as we focus on that, we generate more growth.

So neither he who plants nor he who waters is anything,
but only God who gives the growth.
1 Corinthians 3:7

REFLECTION

WHAT SINS OR ERRORS DO YOU FIND MOST DIFFICULT TO ADMIT?

September 7

The Time Is Now.
The Place Is Wherever You Are.

...for you do not know what a day may bring forth.
Proverbs 27:1

Today you have more experience than you ever have had before. Today, you have more maturity than you ever have had before. Forget your weaknesses. Do not dwell on past mistakes; learn from them and move on.

Your life up until this very moment has been preparing you for today. Listen for God's voice, love unconditionally, let God do the work.

Begin to know Him now and never finish the process.

In that day you will know that I am in my Father,
and you in me, and I in you.
John 14:21

For you yourselves know well that the day of the Lord
will come like a thief in the night.
1 Thessalonians 5:2

REFLECTION

WHAT OPPORTUNITIES DO YOU SEE TODAY
THAT DID NOT EXIST A YEAR AGO? A MONTH AGO?

September 8

Prayer Changes Things

"Truly, truly, I say to you, if you ask anything of the Father,
he will give it to you in my name."
John 16:23

There are a few simple rules about prayer:

- Until you ask, the answer is always "no."
- When you ask, expect an answer.
- There are only three possible answers from God:
  - Yes.
  - Not Yet.
  - I have something better in mind.

Prayer does change things. Be aware of how faithful prayers make changes not just in us spiritually but also even in our physical bodies. When we see the presence of God in our circumstances, we change trouble into harmony. Our bodies, our circumstances, and even the universe itself, respond to our thoughts reflecting our sincere belief.

The fruit of the righteous is a tree of life.
Proverbs 11:30

REFLECTION

HOW DO YOU PRAY? WHAT DO YOU PRAY FOR?
HOW DO YOU PERCEIVE PRAYERS ARE ANSWERED?

September 9

The Power of Your Tongue

Life and death are in the power of the tongue,
and those who love it will eat its fruits.
Proverbs 18:21

...the tongue of the wise brings healing.
Proverbs 12:18

What we say and how we say it have a lasting impact in our lives and the lives of others. When we speak truthfully and lovingly, there is no need to be concerned about the results. Even if the truth may be painful to others, we should speak truthfully and lovingly or not speak at all.

Truthful lips endure forever, but a lying tongue is but for a moment.
Proverbs 12:19

REFLECTION

WHAT SPECIFIC SCRIPTURES HAVE SPOKEN TO YOU THIS MONTH? WHY?

September 10

Get On with It

Rise, let us be going...
Matthew 26:46

In this Matthew reading, the disciples were supposed to be on watch while Jesus was in the Garden of Gethsemane praying. He came from the garden and found His disciples asleep. He did not scold them for their failure to watch but told them to get up and get on with what needed to be done, because the hour was at hand.

Even when we have failed in some way, our lesson from Jesus is "let us be going" on to the business at hand, glorifying God, doing the work we have been given, using the talents we have been blessed with.

REFLECTION

WHAT OR WHO DO YOU DEPEND ON?
WHAT PERSON, SITUATION, OR CONDITION IN YOUR LIFE
HAVE YOU NOT "MOVED ON" FROM?

September 11

Optimism vs. Faith

A faithful person will abound with blessings...
Proverbs 28:20

*Faith is the assurance of things hoped for,
the conviction of things not seen...*
Hebrews 11:1

Cheap optimism is not spiritual. Saying everything will be all right while ignoring the facts of our situation or the consequences of our actions accomplishes nothing positive. We must realize things for what they are and be open to the presence of God to help guide us to a better place. That is faith. We are assured of God's presence, real and active in our lives, even when we feel alone.

REFLECTION

HOW HAS GOD DELIVERED COMFORT TO YOU IN TIMES OF STRESS?

September 12

In That Day

"In that day you will ask nothing of me."
John 16:23

"In that day" we reach a level of understanding where we do not need to ask questions. This is when we are so sure of God's work in our lives that we do not challenge circumstances with human intellect. This does not mean that we have all the answers. This means we are completely comfortable with God's results, and we have no personal, selfish agenda.

Submission to a life like Christ's is simple, but not easy. There is no long list of requirements, no need to set and accomplish goals. The only requirements are total submission with the knowledge that God is at work in His Creation and we as His children are meant to accomplish His purpose.

Wherever you are, whatever you are experiencing, now is the time to accept the fact that you are totally accepted, just the way that you are, and believe that "… the Father himself loves you, because you have loved me and have believed that I came from the Father" (John 16:27).

"… For my yoke is easy, and my burden is light."
Matthew 11:30

REFLECTION

WHAT DO YOU THINK "IN THAT DAY MEANS"?

September 13
God's First Improvement

Then the Lord God said, "It is not good that the man should be alone;
I will make him a helper fit for him."
Genesis 2:18

"Loneliness is the first thing which God's eye named not good."
John Milton

After creating the heavens and the earth, plants, animals, and man, God's first improvement was to create woman.

If man is the head, woman is the crown...the crown of the visible
creation. The woman was made out of a rib from Adam's side; not
made out of his head to rule over him; not out of his feet to be
trampled upon by him, but out of his side to be equal with him,
under his arm to be protected, and near his heart to be beloved.
Matthew Henry, Commentary in One Volume

REFLECTION

THINK OF A WOMAN WHO WAS PARTICULARLY
IMPORTANT TO YOU. WHY WAS SHE IMPORTANT?

September 14

Others Are More Important

Do nothing from selfishness or conceit,
but in humility count others better than yourselves.
Philippians 2:3

Other people are on their own paths, and we are on the path placed before us. With genuine humility we can learn and grow at our own rate, sometimes providing direction to others and other times receiving directions. It is not our purpose to compare our paths.

Looking out for "number one" may lead us to actions that are less than honorable and results that are less than perfect. Looking at the lives of others and learning from their experiences can provide positive direction for us. As we learn and grow we may also provide examples for others to follow in the process. Those results are in God's control.

Following God's direction, maintaining humility, and accepting our conditions all require a lot of work on our part. When we do this work, we really do not have time to judge others.

"Therefore do not be anxious about tomorrow,
for tomorrow will be anxious for itself."
Matthew 6:34

REFLECTION

IN WHAT AREAS OF YOUR LIFE DO YOU NEED TO BE MORE HUMBLE?

September 15

Slow Down

...he who makes haste with his feet misses his way.
Proverbs 19:2

There is nothing better for a man than that he should eat and drink, and find enjoyment in his toil. This, also, is from the hand of God; for apart from him who can eat or who can have enjoyment? For to the man who pleases him God gives wisdom and knowledge and joy...
Ecclesiastes 2:24-26

There is nothing worth worrying about. Worry drains our energy and accomplishes nothing. Worry only prevents peace of mind.

Our spirit, our soul, is going to live forever. There is plenty of time to correct mistakes and mend broken parts. Our purpose in the here and now is to apply our energies to those things that provide spiritual growth and to enjoy the wonderful blessings God has provided for us. Prayer, meditation, studying the word of God, and learning to love are difficult, if not impossible, when worry is the center of our being. Doing His work with joy and appreciating all that He gives us is part of being a child of God. Through these things, our relationship with God grows stronger, and we can know we are blessed to enjoy our time here in His creation.

REFLECTION

WHAT SPECIFIC AREAS OF YOUR LIFE REQUIRE LONG-TERM SOLUTIONS?

September 16

Searching

And you will seek me and find me;
when you seek me with all your heart.
Jeremiah 29:13

God is here, everywhere. Moses saw a burning bush from which God spoke to him. There are burning bushes everywhere from which God speaks to us. It is not His quiet voice that is missing; it is our lack of hearing due to our lack of attention. Negative thoughts and selfish motives distract us and keep us from hearing God's voice.

The blessing of the Lord makes rich, and he adds no sorrow with it.
Proverbs 10:22

REFLECTION

HOW DO YOU VIEW AND EXPERIENCE GOD AS YOUR FATHER?

September 17

Service to Others

I will very gladly spend and be spent for your souls.
2 Corinthians 12:15

Paul's service was not entirely for the love of other people. His service came from his love of the Lord Jesus who commanded that we love one another. If we serve others with a selfish motive, we deceive ourselves and even those around us, but we do not deceive God. When we serve others out of our love of God, God receives that love and turns it back to us. God will be present to help us in the services we give with a loving heart. We are called to love in action.

"The Son of Man came not to be ministered unto, but to minister."
Matthew 20:28

REFLECTION

HOW HAVE YOUR PEERS INFLUENCED YOUR FAITH WALK?

September 18

Procrastination

Look carefully then how you walk, not as unwise men but as wise;
making the most of the time...
Ephesians 5:15-16

"Carpe diem. Seize the day, put no trust in the morrow." These lines were written by the Roman poet Horace in 23 BC and today the words speak volumes to us. A more current aphorism is to "live in the moment." We miss this precious moment when we live waiting for a future moment. Now is the time to do what is important. Now is the time to start doing the right things in all areas of our lives. Now is the time to give and not hold back.

...whereas you do not know about tomorrow.
James 4:14

REFLECTION

WHAT ACTIVITY OR CIRCUMSTANCE DO YOU WANT TO SEIZE TODAY?

September 19
Rejoice in Suffering

…we rejoice in our sufferings, knowing that suffering produces
endurance, and endurance produces character, and character produces
hope, and hope does not disappoint us, because God's love
has been poured into our hearts through the Holy Spirit
which has been given to us.
Romans 5:3-5

We are not to pursue suffering. That becomes a self-righteous act of display and never works to our benefit. When we encounter personal suffering, we should accept it as part of God's plan for our spiritual growth. We should rejoice in it, knowing that God's hand is guiding us to a better place. It is in this suffering that we learn those things we need to know in order to perform our part in accomplishing God's plan.

If you are not wiser today on God's path than you were yesterday, you've only wasted one day. Make wisdom your goal for today. Reviewing, analyzing, and reflecting are good human responses to suffering and unfortunate circumstances. True spiritual growth results from accepting, learning, and acting in faith.

I consider that the sufferings of this present time are not worth
comparing to the glory that is to be revealed to us.
Romans 8:18

We know that in everything God works for good with those who love
him, who are called according to his purpose.
Romans 8:28

REFLECTION

HOW DO YOU THINK YOU SHOULD RESPOND
TO JESUS CHRIST'S SACRIFICE?

September 20

True North

Let no one say when he is tempted, "I am tempted by God"; for God cannot be tempted with evil and he himself tempts no one...
James 1:13

Did you know "true north" differs from magnetic north? True north, the northernmost geographic area of the earth, never changes, but the determination of magnetic north must be calculated because it is affected by the hot metals at the earth's inner core.

The appropriate analogy for this lesson compares our attraction to human matters, or matters of this world, to magnetic north, which is changeable, as opposed to God's truth, which is like true north, never changing. Attraction is simple and human, but it takes correction to find our true north by listening for God's word and following God's will.

Listen now to my voice; I will give you counsel...
Exodus 18:19

REFLECTION

WHEN IS TOLERANCE A VIRTUE? WHEN IS IT A VICE?
HOW DO YOU KNOW THE DIFFERENCE?

September 21

Meditating

Thy word is a lamp to my feet and a light to my path.
Psalm 119:105

Meditating on scripture is a wonderful habit. Proper meditation on scripture allows the word of God to abide in us and us to view the world with spiritual focus.

During meditation, look deeper for how the scripture messages apply to your life and your personal circumstances. Note that in the meditation process you are opening channels of communication, and your message may seem unrelated to the message of the scripture.

Blessed is the man who walks not in the counsel of the wicked,
nor stands in the way of sinners, nor sits in the seat of scoffers;
but his delight is in the law of the Lord, and on his law he meditates
day and night. He is like a tree planted by streams of water,
that yields its fruit in its season, and its leaf does not wither.
In all that he does, he prospers.
Psalm 1:1-3

REFLECTION

WHAT DECISIONS DO YOU FACE TODAY
THAT YOU COULD MEDITATE ON?

AUTUMNAL EQUINOX

The Harvest

... and a time to pluck up what has been planted.
Ecclesiastes 3:3

The autumnal equinox, or fall equinox, is the second period when the sun passes over the equator, creating nearly equal daylight and darkness over all the earth's surface. In the Northern Hemisphere it falls about September 22-23.

This is about the time of harvesting crops that have been growing over the previous months. There are three definitive laws of the harvest:

1- You reap what you sow

2. You reap after you sow

3. You reap more than you sow

This applies to thoughts and beliefs as well as crops and plants. Your thoughts and beliefs—negative or positive—will manifest as experiences.

This is also a great time to reflect on the past few months and readjust toward your goals.

As I have seen, those who plow iniquity
and trouble will reap the same.
Job 4:8

REFLECTION

**WHAT HAVE YOU REAPED AS A RESULT OF THE SEEDS
YOU PLANTED IN MARCH?**

September 22

Trust

"Let not your hearts be troubled; believe in God, believe also in me."
John 14:1

God is constantly giving us opportunities to trust Him. In these instances, it is not a matter of God putting us to the test, but God offering us a chance to see His omnipotent power. In the Gospel of Mark 6:35-37, Jesus instructs His disciples to "give them something to eat." After a day of teaching 5,000 people, Jesus gives His weary disciples a seemingly impossible task. The miracle that followed gave them, and anyone else who wanted to believe, a powerful glimpse of how everything is possible for God.

God gives us these opportunities, gently pushing us outside our comfort zone. When we accept these situations and trust Him, conditions change, people change, and we become better disciples.

REFLECTION

WHEN HAVE YOU SEEN GOD AT WORK?

September 23

Repent

Repent, for the kingdom of heaven is at hand.
Matthew 3:2

Repentance does not mean remembering past mistakes or sins and grieving over them. We are to dwell in the present and do what is right in this moment. Worrying over past mistakes is a refusal to accept God's forgiveness. To repent means to honestly face the fact that a certain action, attitude, or thought was wrong, seek forgiveness, and make a change.

True, honest repentance is an essential step for spiritual progress.

...unless you repent you will all likewise perish.
Luke 13:3

REFLECTION

WHAT TEMPTATIONS DO YOU FACE TODAY?
HOW IS GOD SHOWING YOU A WAY TO OVERCOME THEM?

September 24

Life

Keep your heart with all vigilance; for from it flow the springs of life.
Proverbs 4:23

When the word "life" appears in the Bible, the usual implication is that life is the greatest of all blessings. We are told that "eternal life" is God's greatest reward. Jesus tells us that He is the Light of Life, The Way.

We experience life when we feel free, joyous, and without fear. When the Bible promises us long life, the promise is for long periods of joy and fulfillment. Eternal life is the promise of these things forever.

When we seek more knowledge, wisdom, and understanding of God and God's universe and put God first in our lives, we are paving the way to receive the greatest blessings God has to offer in this life and the life to come.

"...I came that they may have life, and have it abundantly."
John 10:10

REFLECTION

WHAT DOES IT MEAN TO YOU THAT JESUS IS THE LIGHT OF LIFE?

September 25

Wealth

"Do not lay up for yourselves treasures on earth, where moth and
rust consume and where thieves break in and steal, but lay up for
yourselves treasures in heaven, where neither moth nor rust consumes
and where thieves do not break in and steal.
For where your treasure is, there will your heart be also."
Matthew 6:19-21

True wealth includes Christ-like character, love for others, and willful obedience to God's commandments. When we use our God-given talents to accomplish God-given goals, we discover treasure that lasts, treasure whose value far exceeds any earthly wealth. Jesus understood our temptation to focus on earthly things while eternal riches escape our view. In the verses above, He gives us the secret to true wealth and real prosperity.

In his letter to Timothy, Paul gives instruction to the rich in this world:

As for the rich in this world, charge them not to be haughty,
nor to set their hopes on uncertain riches but on God who richly
furnishes us with everything to enjoy. They are to do good,
to be rich in good deeds, liberal and generous, thus laying up for
themselves a good foundation for the future, so that they may take
hold of the life which is life indeed.
1 Timothy 6:17-19

REFLECTION

WHAT OBSTACLES PREVENT US FROM GIVING FREELY?

September 26

Have Faith in Your Own Faith

*"For truly, I say to you, if you have faith as a grain of mustard seed,
you will say to this mountain, 'Move from here to there,'
and it will move; and nothing will be impossible to you."*
Matthew 17:20

If we have enough faith to pray, it will be sufficient. Prayer works. Our willingness to allow God to do His work and our acceptance of the results make all the difference. We can change conditions and circumstances through prayer.

Unfortunately, we cannot always change consequences. Consequences are the results of human and natural laws. Prayer will not prevent gravity from causing you to fall when you jump off of a cliff. Fortunately, we have been educated in the natural laws enough that we do not attempt to violate them without knowing the consequences.

Correct choices are always available to us, and so are incorrect choices. Sometimes, it can be harder to see the consequences of our choices. It is up to us to make the correct choice based on prayer, guidance from what we have learned from scripture. and lessons learned in our faith journey. This is living our faith and having confidence in our faith.

"...do not be faithless but believing."
John 20:27

REFLECTION

WHAT THINGS ARE ATTEMPTING TO BECOME IDOLS IN YOUR LIFE?

September 27

Serving the Lord

Serve the Lord with gladness! Come into his presence with singing!
Psalm 100:2

We are often guilty of dissecting things too much. Like pulling the petals off of a rose, when we dissect the love of God and the joy He can deliver, the beauty seems to disappear. Analysis has its place, but in prayer and meditation, it can diminish our joy in God. He reigns! Be joyful in His presence and doing His work.

The Lord reigns; let the earth rejoice…
Psalm 97:1

REFLECTION

SPEND TIME TODAY THANKING GOD
FOR THE OPPORTUNITY TO DO HIS WORK.

September 28
Things Above

Set your affection on things above, not on things on the earth.
Colossians 3:2

The aim of our lives is God's purpose, not ours. God is using us to fulfill some part of His great plan. We may know only that—or we may discover more. When we seek great things for ourselves, outlining what we think should be His plan for us, we place a barrier to God's use of us. God requires our complete trust. Let go and trust. Carry out your work to the glory of God.

Whatsoever you do, do all to the glory of God.
1 Corinthians 10:31

REFLECTION

DO YOUR ACTIONS AND WORDS TELL THE SAME STORY ABOUT YOU?
WHY OR WHY NOT?

September 29

The Miracle of God's Power

...my speech and my message were not in plausible words of wisdom,
but in demonstration of the Spirit and of power...
1 Corinthians 2:4

Paul delivered many speeches to a wide variety of audiences. He wrote one third of the New Testament. He was a well-trained scholar and an eloquent speaker, but he attributed his message completely to God.

Jesus is a miracle produced only by the power of God. The power of grace and redemption comes through the preaching of the gospel, not the preacher.

REFLECTION

WHEN HAVE YOU FELT GOD SPEAKING THROUGH YOU?

September 30
Build

...Let us rise up and build...
Nehemiah 2:18

God wants us to be part of His plan. We should build our conscious thoughts around embracing God's will. We should be ready to rise up and do whatever we have been called to do. When we create this fundamental readiness as a daily habit, the conditions and materials we need will manifest. In this process, we are continually strengthened through our thoughts, and our spiritual lives are enriched. However, we must take care not to assimilate into our thoughts those things that carry us away from God's will.

...whatever is true, whatever is honorable, whatever is lovely, whatever is gracious, if there is any excellence, if there is anything worthy of praise, think about these things.
Philippians 4:8

REFLECTION

WHAT WILL YOU DO THIS WEEK TO DEMONSTRATE YOUR FAITH?

October 1

But First...

"I will follow you, Lord; but let me first..."
Luke 9:61

In this passage a follower of Jesus expressed willingness to follow but had some other things to do first. Jesus rebuked His follower and insisted that following means resolute abandonment of matters of this world.

There are times when we must totally abandon reason and risk everything on a leap of faith. Sometimes common sense tells us to do or not to do certain things, but deep within, we know that it is time to totally trust God's direction. When we find ourselves in such situations, the best way to begin is to stop and listen. When we are sure of His direction, it is easy. Other times we must act in faith.

When facing a difficult decision or choice, follow the choice that contains the greatest good for all concerned, that is in accordance with what you know to be true about God, and that is in accordance with the teachings of Christ. Then move forward, trusting God entirely, with absolute assurance.

*Jesus said to him, "No one who puts his hand to the plow
and looks back is fit for the kingdom of God."*
Luke 9:62

REFLECTION

WHAT CONSTRAINTS DO YOU FACE IN DEMONSTRATING
YOUR LOVE AND WORSHIP OF GOD?

October 2

Generosity

A generous person will prosper; whoever refreshes others
will be refreshed. (NIV)
Proverbs 11:25

Generosity is the foundation of the universe. The story of creation begins with God giving form to an earth without form. He created light, then heaven, then earth, plants, then day and night, then living creatures. On the sixth day, He created man and woman and gave them dominion over all of it.

God is a giver, and He continues to give. After giving mankind this beautiful world, He gave His Son in order that we might have salvation. Everything is a gift from God.

God wants us to have abundant lives. Our willingness to accept and appreciate His generosity is part of our abundance. The great paradox expressed in the reading from Proverbs is that in our giving or generosity, we prosper.

For as we share abundantly in Christ's sufferings,
so through Christ we share abundantly in comfort too.
2 Corinthians 1:5

REFLECTION

WHAT THINGS OF THIS WORLD ARE MOST IMPORTANT TO YOU? WHY?

October 3
Live Deliberately

...Behold, now is the acceptable time...
2 Corinthians 6:2

Living in the past is counterproductive. It is foolish and futile to live on past realizations without applying our learning from them to the present. Our spiritual life, our realization of God's presence, is here and now.

We can give thanks for yesterday's experiences, good and bad. These experiences provide perspective to help us appreciate today. The story of manna in Exodus 16 is an example of the daily nourishment we receive from God. What we gather will be sufficient. Each of us can gather according to our own understanding. It is not to be hoarded but consumed for our daily sustenance. Tomorrow's nourishment will come at the right time, and we will be able to gather according to our understanding.

The art of living is to live in the present, to make each moment as perfect as possible by realizing that in this moment—here, now—we are God's own expression to this world, to other people, and to God Himself.

He has made everything beautiful in its time...
Ecclesiastes 3:11

REFLECTION

WHAT THINGS ARE YOU TEMPTED TO HOARD? WHY?

October 4

Alignment

…work out your own salvation with fear and trembling.
Philippians 2:12

Look to Jesus. Your conscience and your will are not always in agreement. When you pray, submit and look to Jesus. These two powerful forces align. When we make these moves to work out our path, we find that God is there to help us along the way. When we make God the source of our will, we are firmly and naturally in His will and achieving His results.

Great is our Lord, and abundant in power;
his understanding is beyond measure…
Psalm 147:5

REFLECTION

HOW ARE YOU ALIGNING WITH THE WORLD?
HOW WOULD YOU LIKE TO CHANGE THAT?

October 5
What We Think About Grows

*... make every effort to supplement your faith with virtue, and virtue
with knowledge, and knowledge with self-control, and self-control
with steadfastness, and steadfastness with godliness, and godliness
with brotherly affection, and brotherly affection with love.*
2 Peter 1:5-7

*He has showed you, O man, what is good; and what does the Lord
require of you but to do justice, and to love kindness,
and to walk humbly with your God?*
Micah 6:8

What we think about grows to fill space in our lives. This
applies to our thoughts about our circumstances, our health,
or our finances. It also applies to the people who come into our
lives. Some are easier to love than others, but they are all God's
creatures, and we are blessed to have them in our lives. They are
there for a reason. They might be present to teach us something or
for us to teach them something. And in all cases, they are present
for us to love them as we supplement our faith.

*And we exhort you, brethren, admonish the idlers,
encourage the fainthearted, help the weak, be patient with them all.
See that none of you repays evil for evil,
but always seek to do good to one another and to all.*
1 Thessalonians 5:14-15

"This is my commandment, that you love one another as I have loved you."
John 15:12

REFLECTION

TAKE TIME TO MEDITATE ON TODAY'S 2 PETER SCRIPTURE. HOW CAN YOU APPLY THESE WORDS TO YOUR LIFE?

October 6

Change Your Life
by Changing Your Mind

"Therefore, I tell you, whatever you ask in prayer, believe that you have received it, and it will be yours. And whenever you stand praying, forgive, if you have anything against anyone; so that your Father also who is in heaven may forgive you your trespasses."
Mark 11:24

Our lives reflect our beliefs. If you feel that you are not accomplishing what you want, that you are not making the most of your life, change your beliefs and change your life.

Start by believing in health, prosperity, harmony, and personal satisfaction that can be achieved through your relationship with God. Carry out actions in accordance with learning to believe these things until that belief becomes full and firm. Be confident of God's action in your life when you fully claim your place as a child of God.

"Ask, and it will be given you: seek, and you will find; knock, and the door will be opened to you. For everyone who asks receives, and he who seeks finds, and to him who knocks if will be opened."
Matthew 7:7-8

REFLECTION

WHAT GOOD NEWS DO YOU WANT TO SHARE TODAY?
WHO WILL YOU SHARE IT WITH?

October 7

Commit Your Work

Commit your work to the Lord, and your plans will be established.
Proverbs 16:3

When we think we are in charge, when we make plans and work toward our goals without prayerfully listening to God, the results are always less than what God wants for us. Setting goals and planning are excellent ways to accomplish great things. However, if we really seek fulfillment and peace, the first step is to humbly acknowledge who is in charge and seek to follow His plan for us.

Our competence is from God, who has made us competent to be ministers of a new covenant, not in a written code but in the Spirit; for the written code kills, but the Spirit gives life.
2 Corinthians 3:5-6

All the ways of a man are pure in his own eyes, but the Lord weighs the spirit.
Proverbs 16:2

REFLECTION

HOW WILL YOU DEMONSTRATE YOUR LOVE OF GOD TODAY?

October 8

We're All in This Together

If one member suffers, all suffer together;
if one member is honored, all rejoice together.
1 Corinthians 12:26

When one of us suffers, we all suffer. When we witness suffering, the Holy Spirit generates sympathy in us. The optimum reaction is to seek ways to share the burden with them if possible. Praying for them with genuine sympathy is one way to share the burden, because we are all in this together. When they suffer, we suffer. When they work through their suffering, they usually learn and grow. When we witness this growth, we are rewarded with a feeling of joy for their growth.

Jesus relayed this message as He was suffering on the cross, He said, "Father, forgive them; for they know not what they do." They created suffering for Him and in the process created suffering for everyone who witnessed His situation. Even today, when we consider what Jesus went through, we feel His pain and our guilt. His suffering was a gift to us—a way to salvation and in that we must rejoice and honor the Father and the Son.

Just as we share suffering, so should we freely give honor when one of us is honored. We all grow from the experience of honoring them and rejoicing in their reward. How good it feels to see a worthy person receive the honor due.

REFLECTION

DO YOU REJOICE WHOLEHEARTEDLY
IN THE REWARDING AND BLESSING OF OTHERS?

October 9

Do It

But be doers of the word, and not hearers only…
James 1:22

Spiritual growth comes from practice. By putting the knowledge, awareness, and understanding we have into practice, we experience spiritual growth. What once seemed improbable becomes reality. What we never considered possible begins to happen in our minds and our lives as we experience this spiritual growth and allow God to become the center of our consciousness.

We learn by doing. Regular, consistent practice through prayer, meditation, and reading the word of God generates greater knowledge and understanding and, in the process, gives us spiritual growth with a closer relationship to God. Practice means we can come to serve Him even better!

REFLECTION

NAME THREE WAYS YOU HAVE GROWN SPIRITUALLY
AT THIS POINT IN YOUR JOURNEY.

October 10
Details

His divine power has granted to us all things that pertain to life and godliness, through the knowledge of him who called us to his own glory and excellence, by which he has granted to us his precious and very great promises, that through these you may escape from the corruption that is in the world because of passion and become partakers of the divine nature.
2 Peter 1:3-4

The smallest detail of our obedience has all of the wonderful power of God that the moments of greatest inspiration contain. It is up to us to develop habits that reflect the life that God has placed in us. There are times when the thrill and excitement are not there, but these may be the very times that others see the reflection in us and are moved by it. We are called to do our duty, not out of obligation, but with gratitude. Today's "ho hum" does contain the inspiration and glory of yesterday's "ah ha!" or "WOW" somewhere in it.

For this very reason make every effort to supplement your faith with virtue, and virtue with knowledge.
2 Peter 1:5

REFLECTION

WHAT IS THE MOST IMPORTANT THING YOU EXPECT
FROM SOMEONE ELSE TODAY?

October 11

The Choice Is Yours

...choose this day whom you will serve...
Joshua 24:15

Your circumstances tomorrow will be the result of the choices you make today.

No decision is also a decision, a decision to do nothing. When God provides an opportunity, it is our choice that will make the difference. This choice is between you and God. Consulting with others may provide validation and encouragement, but the choice is between you and God.

The University of North Carolina had long been integrated. However, the local communities, Chapel Hill and Carrboro, still had "white only" business establishments.

A young assistant basketball coach, accompanied by his black pastor, entered a Chapel Hill restaurant and asked to be served. Although this was counter to the social and political customs of the day, it was the right thing to do. The men were served, and the event became a significant part ending segregation in that town.

Years later, the assistant became head basketball coach. Dean Smith's legacy as a coach is legendary. When asked in an interview about his contribution to desegregation, he responded, "You should never be proud of doing what is right, you should just do what's right."

Whoever knows what is right to do and fails to do it, for him it is sin.
James 4:17

REFLECTION

WHAT CRITERIA DO YOU USE WHEN MAKING CHOICES?

October 12

Lay Down Your Life

"Greater love has no man than this,
that a man lay down his life for his friends."
John 15:13

Jesus is not telling us to die for others but rather to lay down our lives for them and for Him. Accepting salvation is "easy" for us because God paid for it. We manifest our appreciation of salvation by laying down our lives, which is very difficult. Carefully and deliberately, we lay down our lives in our daily walk with God. In that process we not only express our thanks to Him but we impact the lives of others with our faithful obedience and conduct.

REFLECTION

WHAT DOES IT MEAN TO YOU TO LAY DOWN YOUR LIFE
FOR OTHERS IN LIGHT OF THIS SCRIPTURE?

October 13

Don't Worry

*And he said to his disciples, "Therefore I tell you,
do not be anxious about your life, what you shall eat,
nor about your body, what you shall put on."*
Luke 12:22

There is always plenty to worry about if you are determined to worry. Financial matters, relationships, job responsibilities, and many other matters demand our attention and sometimes cause us to worry. Many times, we worry about circumstances or results that never occur, but we worry nonetheless. We worry about superficial things and things we cannot control. Take needless worry out of your life. Don't drain your energy.

REFLECTION

WHAT IS THE MOST IMPORTANT THING
YOU DID NOT GET DONE YESTERDAY?

October 14

Rejoice!

Rejoice in the Lord always; again I will say Rejoice!
Philippians 4:4

When we pray, we are having an intimate visit with God. God is always there, and His presence is the same today, tomorrow, and always. His ultimate desire for us is our total happiness, happiness in His will, according to His plan for us. With genuine joy, we should express our understanding of and thanksgiving for God's love.

Thou dost show me the path of life; in thy presence there is fullness of joy, in thy right hand are pleasures for evermore.
Psalm 16:11

REFLECTION

WHAT PEOPLE OR SITUATIONS MAKE YOU FEEL LIKE REJOICING?

October 15

Don't Miss Out

In all your ways acknowledge him,
and he will make straight your paths.
Proverbs 3:6

How do we "acknowledge" God? Acknowledge means recognizing the existence or truth of something or expressing gratitude for something.

When we want to know if we are doing the right thing for God, we can be guided by truthfully answering these questions:

- Am I glorifying God in what I saying and doing?
- Are my thoughts glorifying God?
- Are my relationships glorifying God?
- Am I glorifying God through my career?

If we answer "no" to any of these or similar questions, then changes are in order; the sooner the better. When we "acknowledge" Him in all things, God's greater purpose is glorified through us.

REFLECTION

HOW DO MEANINGFUL SPIRITUAL CONVERSATIONS
HELP US BUILD RELATIONSHIPS WITH EACH OTHER AND WITH GOD?

October 16

Wait

*Wait for the Lord; be strong, and let your heart take courage;
yea, wait for the Lord!*
Psalm 27:14

*...for God is at work in you, both to will and to work for his good
pleasure. Do all things without grumbling or questioning, that you
may be blameless and innocent children of God without blemish in
the midst of a crooked and perverse generation, among whom you
shine as lights in the world...*
Philippians 2:13-15

"Wait" is not an instruction to sit down and see what happens.
It is an exhortation to be steadfast in prayer, fully expecting
an answer and completely willing to follow God's plan. When we
let go of our own agenda and let God do His work in us, our world
is transfigured with peace and joy.

Wait for the Lord, and keep to his way, and he will exalt you...
Psalm 37:34

REFLECTION

HOW DOES THE RUSH OF LIFE'S EXPERIENCES IMPACT YOU NEGATIVELY?

October 17

Vengeance

You shall not take vengeance or bear any grudge against the sons of
your own people, but you shall love your neighbor as yourself:
I am the LORD.
Leviticus 19:18

How often do we really stop to consider the needs of other people? When we do consider the needs of others, how often do we stop short of helping because of self-centered or self-conscious feelings?

Conversely, how often do we have thoughts of vengeance toward those who have offended us?

These thoughts are negative, counterproductive, and destructive.

Just for one day, stop all self-centered and self-conscious thought and genuinely consider the needs of others. Let go of doubt, anxiety, or shyness that keeps you from being open, honest, and caring to everyone you meet. Think about how you feel at the end of the day.

"You shall love the Lord your God with all your heart, and with all
your soul, and with all your strength, and with all your mind;
and your neighbor as yourself."
Luke 10:27

REFLECTION

WHEN HAVE YOU BEEN REJECTED? WHY WAS THIS PAINFUL?

October 18

Limitations?

No wisdom, no counsel, no understanding,
can avail against the Lord.
Proverbs 21:30

God's power is unlimited. God's love for us is boundless. When we have doubt, fear, or insecurity, we are only exhibiting that we do not fully believe these things about God, that we still have work to do on our faith journey. As difficult as it may seem, we must learn to place total faith in the outcome God can provide.

Now faith is the assurance of things hoped for,
the conviction of things not seen.
Hebrews 11:1

REFLECTION

WHERE ARE YOU LIMITING GOD'S POWER IN YOUR LIFE TODAY?
HOW CAN YOU CHANGE THAT?

October 19

Seek First...

*"...seek first his kingdom, and his righteousness,
and all these things shall be yours as well."*
Matthew 6:33

Seek first His kingdom means to keep our sight on the glory promised us eternally by living in righteousness now, following God's word and ways. When we are fixed on spending eternity in God's presence, our path here on earth, full of both joy and trial, has a rich reward at the path's end. Keep the faith. Stay the course.

What we must do is seek the Kingdom in all things. There is an opportunity to learn and grow spiritually when we look for God's presence in all things.

*Trust in the Lord with all your heart, and do not rely on your own insight. In all your ways acknowledge him
and he will make straight your paths.*
Proverbs 3:5-6

REFLECTION

CONSIDER YOUR BIGGEST, MOST URGENT DIFFICULTY.
RELAX AND DRAW A DEEP BREATH. LOOK FOR THE PARADOX
IN THAT DIFFICULTY. WHAT ADVICE WOULD YOU GIVE
TO SOMEONE YOU LOVED WHO WAS IN THE SAME SITUATION?
HOW WOULD YOU TELL THEM TO DEAL WITH THIS SITUATION?

October 20

Testing

*Consider it pure joy, my brothers and sisters, whenever you face trials
of many kinds, because you know that the testing
of your faith produces perseverance.*
James 1:2-3

Tests are an important part of the learning process. Teachers give tests to determine what the students have learned. Test results indicate a student's readiness to progress to the next lesson.

The tests of life offer us an opportunity to grow and progress to greater understanding. We are tested in our faith walk because progress will require more faith, and more faith will produce more blessings of knowledge and understanding.

The tests of life can yield results that require more dependence on God and a deeper relationship with Him. We learn what is in accordance with His love and His plan, and we discard the rest.

...test everything; hold fast what is good,
1 Thessalonians 5:21

REFLECTION

WHAT MAKES YOU ANGRY? WHY?

October 21

Doubt and Direction

Cast all your anxieties on him, for he cares about you.
1 Peter 5:7

When in doubt, pray for inspiration and direction. Then thank God for what you are about to discover. When you are afraid, thank God for protection and the knowledge that you are in His hands. When someone is bothering you, ask God to show you His presence in that person and allow you to love that person for being a child of God. When difficult situations cause you true worry, pray for guidance and look for the lesson God wants you to learn. When in transition—and it's all transition—pray for wisdom and understanding. You are on a path to better conditions and greater understanding. Stop, look, listen, and accept it as an adventure.

A man's mind plans his way, but the Lord directs his steps.
Proverbs 16:9

REFLECTION

WHAT DECISIONS ARE YOU FACING THAT REQUIRE WISE COUNSEL?

October 22

Our Light and our Vision

"Do not judge by appearances, but judge with right judgment."
John 7:24

Sometimes life's events are confusing or perplexing. When suffi-cient spiritual growth is attained, there is faith that these events are part of an orderly pattern, a pattern directed toward accomplishing God's plan, even if the pattern is not discernable to human understanding.

Even those who walked with Jesus experienced this confusion.

After this many of his disciples drew back
and no longer went about with him.
John 6:66

You must walk in the light of the vision you have been given using the gifts you have received. Do not to compare yourself to others. Do not measure your gifts against someone else's. Do not judge another's gifts or status or gains. You do not know their path.

You were placed where you are for a reason. Accept the fact that you are totally accepted as you are. He chose you. He loves you through your travels on all the peaks, valleys, and bumps on the path.

REFLECTION

WHAT DOES " JUDGE WITH RIGHT JUDGMENT" MEAN TO YOU?

October 23

Be Strong

*Then David said to Solomon his son, "Be strong and of good courage,
and do it. Fear not, be not dismayed; for the LORD God,
even my God, is with you. He will not fail you or forsake you…"*
1 Chronicles 28:20

At God's direction, King David has given Solomon the formidable task of building the Temple in Jerusalem. Then David gives his son beautiful words of encouragement. The same promises David makes to Solomon on God's behalf are appropriate for any task we undertake on God's path as well.

When we seek God's guidance for tasks, simple or complex, His assurance of constant presence and support is assured. He will not fail or forsake.

*And you, Solomon my son, know the God of your father, and serve
him with a whole heart and with a willing mind…*
1 Chronicles 28:9

REFLECTION

WHAT CURRENT TASK IN YOUR LIFE SEEMS FORMIDABLE TO YOU?
HOW CAN GOD HELP?

October 24

The Wisdom of Solomon

At Gibeon the LORD *appeared to Solomon in a dream by night;*
and God said, "Ask what I shall give you.
1 Kings 3:5

Solomon responds: "I do not know how to go out or come in...
Give thy servant therefore an understanding mind."

Solomon asked for wisdom, and God granted it to him and
we read in scripture that he reigned well for years. However, despite
his early wise and faithful response to God, Solomon allowed his
great wealth and worldly matters to overtake him. He fell away
from God even though God had blessed him so much. Our lesson
from this is to receive the gifts of God with joy and appreciation
and never forget the source of the blessings and make sure to follow
His will.

REFLECTION

WHAT ARE YOU PASSIONATE ABOUT?

October 25

Do It Now

And you shall do what is right and good in the sight of the LORD,
that it may go well with you...
Deuteronomy 6:18

Do now what you know you will have to do some day. When you are ready to allow God to alter your outlook and attitude, He will begin to work within you. God's purpose is that you be correctly related to Him in mind and spirit and then that you share that relationship with other people.

You are not measured by what you say you will do. You are judged and measured by your deeds, not your intentions.

REFLECTION

IN WHAT WAYS HAVE YOU ALLOWED GOD TO ALTER YOUR OUTLOOK?
WHAT DO YOU STILL NEED TO WORK ON?

October 26

Being on the Path

Draw near to God and he will draw near to you.
James 4:8

One is either on the spiritual path or the world's path. According to Emmet Fox, an influential early twentieth-century spiritual thought leader, you are on your spiritual path if you truly:

- give all power to God, in the most literal, practical, matter-of-fact sense.
- believe prayer can do anything.
- believe that your happiness and well-being are vitally important in the eyes of God.
- try to see the presence of God everywhere.
- realize your ideas and beliefs must be expressed in your surroundings, your relationships, and in your activities.
- understand that you are in a spiritual universe, that thoughts are things and that your life is fundamentally the expression of your belief about and in God.

REFLECTION

WHICH PATH ARE YOU ON? HOW DO YOU KNOW THAT?

October 27

By Faith

*By faith Abraham obeyed when he was called to go out to a place
which he was to receive as an inheritance;
and he went out, not knowing where he was to go.*
Hebrews 11:8

There are several Old Testament examples of faith that show the faithful person separating from country, family, or occupation. In a life of faith, we know who is making our decisions. We follow, not sure where we are being led, but loving and trusting God to lead us. Sometimes He leads us to abundance, sometimes His way is through difficulty. Regardless of the experience, He will be present with us. If we walk with Him in love and in faith, our journey will glorify Him.

REFLECTION

HOW DOES YOUR FAITH HELP YOU THROUGH DIFFICULT TIMES?

October 28

Living Water

*"He who believes in me, as the scripture has said,
'Out of his heart shall flow rivers of living water.'"*
John 7:38

The "living water" is what He pours into this world through us. When we believe in God, listen to His voice, and follow God's direction, not only do we live lives of fulfillment but we offer the same to others.

It is not that God makes us perfect specimens but that He develops us to make the world a better place. God's training is often challenging, but always rewarding. We do not always see the rewards, and we cannot always measure the success of our lives but God can.

REFLECTION

WHAT DOES WALKING WITH THE LORD MEAN TO YOU AT THIS POINT IN YOUR JOURNEY?

October 29

Active Waiting

*Happy is the man who listens to me, watching daily at my
gates, waiting beside my doors.*
Proverbs 8:34

Where do I go? What do I do? How will I...? All are questions we ask when we know that we want to follow God's direction. Sometimes, we are simply called to participate in active waiting, praying and waiting for God to answer our prayers. When we are in active waiting, it is very important to clear our minds of worldly clutter.

Active waiting also means preparing in anticipation of the prayer being answered. If we pray for rain, we need to have an umbrella. If we pray for direction in a certain area, we need to use our discernment and experience on God's path to prepare for God's response. Having an open mind for direction can bear fruit we never anticipated

*Remember your leaders, who spoke the word of God to you. Consider
the outcome of their way of life and imitate their faith.*
Hebrews 13:7

REFLECTION

WHAT ARE YOU ACTIVELY WAITING ON TODAY?

October 30

Don't Look Now

And Peter answered him, "Lord, if it is you, bid me come to you on the water." He said, "Come." So Peter got out of the boat and walked on the water and came to Jesus; but when he saw the wind, he was afraid, and beginning to sink he cried out, "Lord, save me."
Matthew 14:28-30

Peter asked Jesus to say "come," and the Lord did. In fact, Jesus is constantly calling us to come to Him.

When we hear the voice, when we see God's presence, it is time to let go of earthly conditions and follow Him. When we abandon ourselves in faith, our perspective changes and so do the conditions that surround us.

The more we focus on hearing God's voice, the more clearly we hear it. Our recognition of His voice increases with practice. Letting go is up to us. Recklessly departing from earthly conditions is not for the faithless, but for those who come in complete humility with total faith. And even if we momentarily allow fear to overcome, He will reach out to save us.

There is great gain in godliness with contentment.
1 Timothy 6:6

REFLECTION

WHAT DOES GOD'S VOICE SOUND LIKE TO YOU?

October 31

Assurance

Now faith is the assurance of things hoped for,
the conviction of things not seen.
Hebrews 11:1

Do not dissect the Love of God. Accept it and feel it! This is faith and hope. God is Love. We cannot grasp the fullness of God or His love. What we can do is grow our faith daily that God, though unseen, is present always, and He will be our refuge and comfort in times of trouble. We cannot know how He will answer our petitions in the moment, but we can have faith in His ultimate goodness, mercy, and righteousness in His long-range plans.

Let the righteous rejoice in the Lord, and take refuge in him!
Psalm 64:10

REFLECTION

HOW DO YOU "FIT IN" WITH YOUR PEERS?
HOW WOULD YOU LIKE TO CHANGE THAT?

November 1

The Prisons of This World

But about midnight Paul and Silas were praying and
singing hymns to God, and the prisoners were listening to them...
Acts 16:25

Paul and Silas were in prison. They had been seized, beaten, and imprisoned after local business people found them to be a threat to business. They were placed in the inner prison, and their feet were fastened in the stocks. They were in a situation many would call hopeless, but they found cause to pray and sing hymns. They knew that even there, God was with them. God is always at work, working in our lives and the lives of others around us, to accomplish His purpose.

When we choose to look for God and praise Him in all things, we find His blessings in even the most negative situations. Paul and Silas chose to praise Him and sing hymns rather than focus on their plight.

REFLECTION

ADVERSITY IS REAL. HOW DO YOU REMAIN HOPEFUL IN ADVERSITY?

November 2

Our Impact on Others
in Similar Conditions

...and the prisoners were listening to them...
Acts 16:25

You never know who is listening. Others see and hear us, and when we least expect it, we are having an impact on their lives.

Paul and Silas were having an impact on the lives of their fellow prisoners because they were praying and singing in spite of adversity. They did not know God's plan, but they knew God was at work and was worthy of praise.

God was at work in the lives of Paul, Silas, and through them, all of the other prisoners. Paul and Silas were worshiping God through hymns. They were living their faith in God under harsh conditions and their actions went to the hearts of fellow prisoners. In a similar way, even our daily actions and casual conversations can have intended and untended impact on those around us. When we have professed as Christians, those actions reflect on our faith. The question is, do they glorify God? Are we walking in the path of the Lord?

In this account of Paul and Silas, God wasn't through yet.

...and suddenly there was a great earthquake, so that the foundations of the prison were shaken; and immediately all the doors were opened and everyone's fetters were unfastened.
Acts 16:26

REFLECTION

**HOW HAVE PAST TRIALS, TRIBULATIONS,
AND CHALLENGES CHANGED YOU?**

November 3

It's All Part of God's Plan

When the jailer awoke and saw that the prison doors were open,
he drew his sword and was about to kill himself, supposing that the
prisoners had escaped. But Paul cried with a loud voice,
"Do not harm yourself, for we are all here."
Acts 16:27-28

Paul knew that he was in the right place, doing what he was supposed to do. He was where God had placed him for a special reason. He was there to witness to the jailer, which he did. The jailer's response was to ask what he must do to be saved. Paul told him to believe in the Lord Jesus and he and his household would be saved.

This entire scenario, from the capture of Paul and Silas through their imprisonment and the earthquake, was part of God's plan. Saving the jailer and his family was one purpose. Perhaps there were others, prisoners and jailers, who were saved at the same time. God has His plans.

REFLECTION

REMEMBER A TIME WHEN YOU HAD A BROKEN SPIRIT.
NOW, LOOK BACK FROM TODAY'S PERSPECTIVE.
WHAT DID YOU LEARN?

November 4

Winter

*While the earth remains, seedtime and harvest, cold and heat,
summer and winter, day and night, shall not cease.*
Genesis 8:22

The seasons of the year are often compared to the seasons of our lives. Preparation and planting in spring, growth in summer, and harvest in the fall all have appropriate applications to the phases of our lives.

Winter weather in many areas includes snow. Many choose to remain indoors when this weather comes. However, notice the joy and excitement children express when they see snow. It's all in the viewpoint! We can choose to accept pleasure or misery in weather conditions—or in life—by choice of our viewpoint.

*He changes times and seasons; he removes kings and sets up kings;
he gives wisdom to the wise and knowledge
to those who have understanding...*
Daniel 2:21

REFLECTION

HOW DO YOU FEEL "CHILDLIKE" AS YOU DRAW CLOSER TO GOD?

November 5

Telling Your Story

And he told them many things in parables.
Matthew 13:3

Jesus taught with parables. These parables often related to the day-to-day circumstances in the lives of His followers. This made it easy for His listeners to relate to the stories. In an agrarian society, His parables concerning planting, growing, and harvesting provided excellent parallels.

The deeper meanings were readily apparent to those who were seeking spiritual truth.

"He who has ears, let him hear."
Matthew 13:9

To those not seeking spiritual truth, the parables Jesus told were simply good stories.

"With them indeed is fulfilled the prophecy of Isaiah which says:
'You shall indeed hear but never understand,
and you shall indeed see but never perceive.'"
Matthew 13:14

REFLECTION

HOW WILL YOU BLESS OTHERS TODAY? WHO WILL THAT BE?

November 6

Stepping Stones

*For it is precept upon precept, precept upon precept, line upon line,
line upon line, here a little, there a little...*
Isaiah 28:10

Consider every experience as a stepping stone. We are not today
what we will ultimately become. Our experiences today are
to prepare us for tomorrow. If we were to move immediately to
tomorrow's experiences, we would not gain full benefit, or we may
miss the benefit entirely if we do not learn and grow from today's
circumstances.

Today, open your eyes to current circumstances, acquaintanc-
es, and events. Look at your conditions today as if they contain
spiritual lessons with deep spiritual meaning. With this perspective and open acceptance of today's conditions for what they are,
prepare yourself for the greater things of tomorrow. In the process,
demonstrate to others your faith and confidence.

*...for once you were darkness, but now you are light in the Lord;
walk as children of light...*
Ephesians 5:8

REFLECTION

HOW CAN YOU SHOW YOUR APPRECIATION TO THOSE
WHO HELPED YOU CONNECT WITH GOD?

November 7

Tend My Sheep

"He said to him, "Tend my sheep."
John 21:16

Jesus, talking to His disciple John, tells him to "tend" His sheep. Who are His sheep? Everyone we encounter is one of His sheep. How are we to tend His sheep? By loving them, caring for them, feeding them with spiritual encouragement, and demonstrating to them with our daily conduct. Our responsibility is to guide others in such a manner that God may speak to them. We encourage and nurture with love and acceptance. Their response will change their lives.

REFLECTION

WHO ARE THE SHEEP IN YOUR LIFE?

November 8

Rejection

*Blessed be God, because he has not rejected my prayer
or removed his steadfast love from me!*
Psalm 66:20

Being rejected is part of the human experience. We all suffer being rejected by this world at one time or another. Jesus certainly had this human experience, but it did not keep Him from listening to His Father's voice and following His Father's direction.

When we are rejected, our response not only reflects our faith but also becomes a beacon to those who reject us. Our example may cause others to change, or it may not, but they are probably watching closely for our response. How we handle their rejection is also being observed by other people. More important than this, we are demonstrating our belief that we are totally accepted by the only One who matters: God. Our reflection of God's acceptance of us as we are is planting a seed somewhere.

The Lord has heard my supplication; the Lord accepts my prayer.
Psalm 6:9

REFLECTION

HOW DO YOU HANDLE REJECTION? HOW DOES THIS IMPACT OTHERS?

November 9

Let It Go

*But a man of God came to him and said, "O king, do not let the
army of Israel go with you, for the L*ORD* is not with Israel,
with all these Ephraimites."*
2 Chronicles 25:7

Amaziah, king of Judah, hired 100,000 troops to grow his army.
A prophet of God appeared after he had hired them and told
Amaziah that they were men who had abandoned God and relying
on these men in battle would be in opposition to trusting in God.
Meanwhile, Amaziah had paid them and was wondering what to
do about all the money he had spent.

And Amaziah said to the man of God, "But what shall we do
about the hundred talents which I have given to the army of Israel?"
The man of God answered, "The LORD is able to give you much
more than this." The king decided to let it go and trust in God.

All of us at one time or another are guilty of holding on to
an attitude or a possession that runs contrary to trusting in God.
Unfortunately, the result is rarely satisfying. "Let it go" is good advice. When the result belongs to God, there is no regret. We know
what is right, but it is often difficult to do what is right.

*Trust in the L*ORD* with all your heart,
and do not rely on your own insight.*
Proverbs 3:5

REFLECTION

WHAT PRINCIPLES DO YOU LIVE BY THAT LEAD TO WISDOM?

November 10

God's Peace

Have no anxiety about anything, but in everything by prayer and supplication with thanksgiving let your requests be made known to God. And the peace of God, which passes all understanding, will keep your hearts and your minds in Christ Jesus.
Philippians 4:6-7

These two verses clearly, concisely, and completely describe the atmosphere of a life where we acknowledge God's dominion. Paul introduces this message with Philippians 4:4-5: "Rejoice in the Lord always; again I will say, Rejoice. Let all men know your forbearance. The Lord is at hand. Have no anxiety about anything, but in everything by prayer and supplication with thanksgiving let your requests be made known to God."

Paul then tells us how to find that peace with Philippians 4:8: "Finally, brethren, whatever is true, whatever is honorable, whatever is just, whatever is pure, whatever is lovely, whatever is gracious, if there is any excellence, if there is anything worthy of praise, think about these things."

Our thoughts control our lives. Our emotions, our attitudes toward ourselves and others, and our actions reflect the things we think about. If we want peace, love, and prosperity to come into our lives, we start with thoughts of peace, love, and prosperity.

REFLECTION

WHAT ARE THREE WAYS YOU CAN ADD MORE PEACE TO YOUR LIFE?

November 11

Don't Waste It

...whereas you do not know about tomorrow. What is your life?
For you are a mist that appears for a little time and then vanishes.
James 4:14

Our human lives have a beginning and an end. We have no choice about the beginning. When and where we are born are in God's hands. We have no choice about who our parents will be or the conditions into which we will be born.

The end is another matter entirely. When we reach our ultimate human destination, we will have lived a span of years where the circumstances we encountered were largely a result of our choices. Did we make good choices? Did we practice care and concern for others? Did we listen for God's direction? Did we use our talents to the best of our ability? Did we learn from life's lessons along the way? Were we thankful for the blessings in our life? Did we claim our place as a child of God? The answers to those questions will determine what happens to us at the end of our life. Will we reflect in peace or in pain?

Do not wait for tomorrow to make good answers to these questions. Let today and every day be days you live life in light of Christ's teachings and the word of God!

"If we fully comprehended the brevity of life, our greatest desire
would be to please God and serve one another."
Dr. James Dobson

REFLECTION

**HOW DO YOU THINK GOD WILL BE WORKING THROUGH YOU
TODAY TO ACCOMPLISH HIS PLAN?**

November 12

Train to Win

Do you not know that in a race all the runners compete,
but only one receives the prize? So run that you may obtain it.
1 Corinthians 9:24

If you have ever trained for something, you know it starts out slow and easy. As you continue to train, the training becomes more challenging and less like fun and more like hard work. But it is training that separates the winners from the rest, the professionals from the amateurs.

Training to be the person God wants us to be is similar. The training gets more challenging as we progress, but the discipline and practice we gain give us a different perspective. The rewards may not come as quickly as a trophy for winning a race. In fact, we may not see a physical reward for a long time, if at all. However, discipline and practice, prayer and meditation, studying scripture and listening for God's voice provide rewards that, in the long term, are satisfying and worth the training because they build a deeper relationship with God.

I have fought the good fight, I have finished the race,
I have kept the faith.
2 Timothy 4:7

REFLECTION

WHY DO YOU THINK IT IS IMPORTANT TO "BE IN TRAINING"
TO DEEPEN YOUR RELATIONSHIP WITH GOD?

November 13

God Can Use You

Come, I will send you to Pharaoh that you may bring forth my people,
the sons of Israel, out of Egypt.
Exodus 3:10

God is talking to Moses from the burning bush. Moses was a
murderer, a fugitive, and a less than impressive public speaker. He was certainly apprehensive about being able to accomplish
the formidable task God was giving him, yet look what he accomplished with God's help.

No matter who you are, no matter what talents you possess or
don't possess, God can use you for His glory. Accept the challenge
and proceed. God will be with you.

But I will be with you; and this shall be the sign for you, that I have
sent you: when you have brought forth the people out of Egypt, you
shall serve God upon this mountain.
Exodus 3:12

REFLECTION

WHAT CIRCUMSTANCE ARE YOU READY NOW TO
LET GO OF AND TRUST GOD TO HANDLE?

November 14

It Is No Accident

Ever since the creation of the world, his invisible nature,
namely, his eternal power and deity, has been clearly perceived
in the things that have been made.
Romans 1:20

The beauty of His creation is no accident. He made this beautiful world for us to enjoy. In the process, He provided clues in the complexity of His creation that allow us to become better acquainted with Him. God constantly and consistently reveals Himself to us in many ways. Unfortunately, we become distracted by the *world* and miss the beauty of the *earth*.

A quiet walk can renew the spirit and refresh our perspective on the things that really matter. A connection with God's creation can fill us with hope as we see the beauty, breadth, and power in His work.

REFLECTION

WHAT DOES BEING IN NATURE REVEAL TO YOU ABOUT GOD?

November 15

We Are Created for Good Works

For we are his workmanship created in Christ Jesus for good works,
which God prepared beforehand, that we should walk in them.
Ephesians 2:10

We were created by God to do good and through Christ we are redeemed to carry out those good works. Christ showed us good works and right living and called us to love God and to love one another—to do what we were created to do.

While it is always good to love and serve others, it is also true that they often want to respond to us in a similar fashion. If not, the pleasure is still yours, and you never know what the long-term effect may be or what surprises may be in store as a result of your kindness.

REFLECTION

HOW ARE YOU BEING WHO YOU WERE CREATED TO BE?

November 16
The Fruit of the Spirit

Humble yourselves therefore under the mighty hand of God....
Cast all your anxieties on him, for he cares about you. Be sober, be
watchful. Your adversary the devil prowls around like a roaring lion,
seeking someone to devour. Resist him, firm in your faith...
1 Peter 5:6-9

The world and the forces of evil will seek to exploit our weaknesses in order to prevent us from accomplishing God's purposes for us. We are easily drawn into spiritual lethargy, immorality, and pride. Resisting can be difficult, because we are human with human weakness.

But the fruit of the Spirit is love, joy, peace, patience, kindness,
goodness, faithfulness, gentleness, self-control;
against such there is no law.
Galatians 5:22-23

If we practice the attributes of the fruits of the Holy Spirit, we not only strengthen ourselves to resist the adversary but we are better able to accept the fact that we are totally accepted by a generous and loving God. Recognizing our acceptance by God leads us ever higher on our spiritual path.

REFLECTION

**WHAT FRUIT OF THE SPIRIT DO YOUR STRIVE TO EXEMPLIFY
IN YOUR WORK FOR GOD? WHY?**

Understanding vs. Thinking We Understand

A fool takes no pleasure in understanding,
but only in expressing his opinion.
Proverbs 18:2

Opinions are just that—opinions. When we speak hastily or speak without understanding or deliver thoughtless words, we can do harm to ourselves and to others. Speak with care. Seek guidance when you speak of spiritual matters. Seek to understand. If you must deliver an opinion, let it be well-reasoned and righteous.

REFLECTION

WHAT STEPS CAN YOU TAKE TO MAKE SURE
YOU DO NOT SPEAK IN HASTE AND WITHOUT UNDERSTANDING?

November 18
Do Not Look Back

*Jesus said to him, "No one who puts his hand to the plow
and looks back is fit for the Kingdom of God."*
Luke 9:62

Your journey to reach the Kingdom of God should be forward moving only. It may not be in a straight line, but your eyes should ever be on the goal, not on what is behind you.

Likewise, on your journey, do not start a plan unless you really believe it is worthwhile. If you are convinced it is worthwhile, do not rest until you have brought it to fruition.

*Let your eyes look directly forward,
and your gaze be straight before you.*
Proverbs 4:25

REFLECTION

WHY DO YOU THINK IT IS IMPORTANT TO LOOK FORWARD
IN YOUR JOURNEY WITH GOD AND NOT DWELL IN THE PAST?

November 19
It's Results That Count

Whoever loves discipline loves knowledge...
Proverbs 12:1

At first, it can be difficult to discipline ourselves to set aside time to spend with God. Making a place in our daily lives for scripture study, quiet time, and prayer time can seem like an impossible goal, but we can do it. And if we discipline ourselves to make the time, our pleasure in this time will grow as will the strength of our relationship with God and our knowledge of His path for us.

When we love to learn more about God, when we open our hearts to His love, our joy grows and peace and contentment surround us.

REFLECTION

CONSIDER THE WAYS YOUR LOVE FOR GOD HAS GROWN SO FAR
THROUGH THIS YEAR OF DEVOTIONAL STUDIES.
HOW HAS THIS AFFECTED YOUR DAILY LIFE?

November 20

What Do You See?

He who has a bountiful eye will be blessed
for he shares his bread with the poor.
Proverbs 22:9

When we take our eyes off of our own circumstances and seek ways to love and serve others, we often discover things we never expected. In this season for Thanksgiving, it is wonderful to take the time to count and celebrate our many blessings and to be thankful for all we have, but it is a good time to consider how to help others who are in need—to share from our bounty. There is always someone who has less than you do. Look around you. Reach out. Share your bread.

REFLECTION

HOW WILL YOU "SHARE YOUR BREAD" THIS HOLIDAY SEASON?

November 21

True Place

*...we, though many, are one body in Christ
and individually members of one another.*
Romans 12:5

According to Mark Twain, the two most important days of your life are the day you were born and the day you find out why you were born.

Each of us has a place within the body of Christ and a role that we were specifically designed to play. In order to find our correct place, we must first find out what we are designed to do. Sometimes, we need to discover and accept what we are not designed to do.

Christian perfection is not human perfection. Thoughts centered about yourself hinder your usefulness. Focus on your God given talents and use them to obey God's call. God is getting you to your true place to do His work you were born to do!

REFLECTION

WHAT IS GOD CALLING YOU TO DO TODAY? FOR THE LONG TERM?

November 22

Hope

The hope of the righteous ends in gladness, but the expectation of the wicked comes to nought.
Proverbs 10:28

Each of us has a personal meaning for "hope." To many of us, hope is a shallow expectation, a wish that may or may not be fulfilled.

Biblical hope is a different matter. Hope in the Bible is a future reality, something we are promised that is not yet accomplished. Biblical hope is a future joy, a certainty, not a wish. God is always true to His word. He is always with us and He has a place for us everlastingly with Him if we choose to claim it.

Let us hold fast the confession of our hope without wavering, for he who promised is faithful...
Hebrews 10:23

REFLECTION

WHAT DOES THE HOPE OF ETERNAL LIFE MEAN TO YOU?

November 23

Mothers

When Jesus saw his mother, and the disciple whom he loved standing near, he said to his mother, "Woman, behold, your son!"
John 19:26

Mary, the mother of Jesus, is a significant part of His ministry. She appears at special moments to underscore His work. His first public miracle, turning water to wine at the wedding feast at Cana, was at her request. She was there to teach Him as he grew up, support Him, and even to watch Him die.

Mothers provide wonderful support, but often remain in the background. They have moments of being proud, feeling loved, and feeling hurt. They often suffer in silence while continuing to be supportive of their children.

Mary, as the mother of Jesus, did all of those earthly things for Him that we don't think about. She fed Him, changed His diapers, helped Him learn to walk, and nursed His childhood hurts. She was also there in His final moments, unable to rescue Him, but still there.

So the soldiers did this. But standing by the cross of Jesus were his mother, and his mother's sister, Mary the wife of Clopas, and Mary Magdalene.
John 19:25

REFLECTION

WHO IS SOMEONE WHO HAS MADE YOU A BETTER PERSON? HOW DID THEY INFLUENCE YOU?

November 24

Meditation

but his delight is in the law of the LORD, and on his law,
he meditates day and night.
Psalm 1:2

Delight in reading and meditating on God's word leads to a fruitful life. The practice and process of meditation enables discernment. Pleasing God is our purpose. When we please God, we are not necessarily pleasing the world. God's perspective is revealed in His words, but a quick, cursory reading does not always reveal the total truth. Meditation on His words enables God to reveal His truth to us—sometimes slowly, sometimes in a flash, sometimes in a moment of need.

Meditation helps discernment. In discernment, we learn what our true heart's desire is. That desire is our purpose. Through meditation and discernment, we can find spiritual strength to build up what we want and rid our consciousness of those things we do not want.

Create mental equivalents of your heart's desire. Think with clarity and purpose. Continue seeking discernment to make sure you are on the path meant for you. When a negative thought enters, substitute the positive details of your desire that you have discerned through your meditation. Keep your focus on the desire God has put in your heart—your purpose.

Acquaint now thyself with him and be at peace;
thereby good shall come to thee.
Job 22:21

The fear of the Lord is the beginning of wisdom,
and the knowledge of the Holy One is insight.
Proverbs 9:10

REFLECTION

CHOSE ONE SCRIPTURE THAT ESPECIALLY SPEAKS TO YOU
AND TAKE TIME TO MEDITATE ON IT FIVE MINUTES A DAY
FOR THE NEXT FIVE DAYS.
BE AWARE OF NEW MEANINGS IN THE PASSAGE
AS YOU CONTINUE YOUR MEDITATION.

November 25

How to Deal with Negativity

What you have learned and received and heard and seen in me, do;
and the God of peace will be with you.
Philippians 4:9

A negative thought is any thought of failure, trouble, disappointment, jealousy, sickness, accident, limitation of ourselves or others. We all have negative thoughts. It is not the thoughts, but how we choose to deal with them that really matters. A good remedy is to deal with negative thoughts quickly and replace them with positive thoughts.

Release the emotion caused by the negative thought before it lodges and grows in the mind and heart. Replace that negative emotion with a thought of thankfulness or a moment gratitude or an appreciation of something around you or take a moment to say a short prayer. Paul admonished the people at Philippi to learn from what they received, saw, and heard from him to receive God's peace. "Teach" yourself to replace negative with positive through prayer, scripture, and practice, and you will find more peace, joy, and wellbeing in your life!

REFLECTION

WHAT IS THE HARDEST NEGATIVE EMOTION FOR YOU TO DEAL WITH?
WHAT POSITIVE EMOTION CAN YOU USE TO REPLACE IT?

November 26

Fall Seven Times, Get Up Eight

...for a righteous man falls seven times, and gets up again
but the wicked are overthrown by calamity.
Proverbs 24:16

Wherever you are, whatever you are doing, you are there to learn. Life throws difficult situations at us for a reason. In every difficulty, there is at least one lesson. When we focus on the difficulty, what we focus on grows. The problem grows and assumes proportions that make us shrink in fear and defeat.

When we face adversity squarely, things change, usually for the better. Do not try to explain them away. Do not dream of changing the past. Forget what has happened and focus on what you are going to make happen. When you fall down, get up and start again.

REFLECTION

WHAT DIFFICULT SITUATION ARE YOU FACING TODAY THAT NEEDS GOD'S WISDOM?

November 27

Private Prayer

*"But when you pray, go into your room and shut the door and
pray to your Father who is in secret; and your Father
who sees in secret will reward you."*
Matthew 6:6

Do you have a special place? Do you have a place where you can pray and meditate without interruption or worldly intrusion? If not, now is a great time to find one.

When you enter your special place, you may find that is where you can get closest to God. Although God is everywhere all of the time, and speaking to you constantly, often it is when you deliberately depart from daily intrusions and allow God to speak to you without interruption that you can hear His voice best. God loves to manifest His grace and glory. Allow yourself to witness these manifestations by removing the cares of this world. Your special place can signal to your mind, heart, and spirit to step away from "busyness" and be ready to commune with your heavenly Father.

"But seek first his kingdom…"
Matthew 6:33

REFLECTION

ARE YOU AWARE OF THE HOLY SPIRIT'S PRESENCE
IN YOUR LIFE EVERY DAY? HOW?

November 28

Don't Pretend

"Woe to you, scribes and Pharisees, hypocrites! For you are like whitewashed tombs, which outwardly appear beautiful, but within they are full of dead men's bones and all uncleanness."
Matthew 23:27

It is all too easy to pretend, to put forth a presence of confidence and piety. This is true for everyone, even that person you think has it all together. We all face difficulties. We all fear failure. We all encounter situations where we feel things are beyond our control. We all feel helpless at one time or another. God is not looking for perfect people. In fact, God knows that there is no such thing as a perfect person on this earth.

God is seeking those who know and understand their need for Him. When we come to terms with our personal need, and as a result see the needs in others, we are freed from our own hypocritical perspective, and we become useful to God for His purposes. It takes courage to be honest with ourselves and others.

Have I not commanded you? Be strong and of good courage; be not frightened, neither be dismayed; for the LORD your God is with you wherever you go.
Joshua 1:9

REFLECTION

WHAT PERSONAL WEAKNESS—PHYSICAL, MENTAL, OR SPIRITUAL—
HAVE YOU BECOME AWARE OF IN YOURSELF THIS WEEK?

November 29
The Sound of Silence

...a man of understanding remains silent.
Proverbs 11:12

Publilius Syrus, a Latin writer of maxims, flourished in the first century BC. He was a Syrian who was brought as a slave to Italy but by his wit and talent he won the favor of his master who freed and educated him. His one sentence maxims included the following observations:

"I have often regretted my speech, never my silence".
Maxim 1070

"Let a fool hold his tongue, and he will pass for a sage."
Maxim 914

"It is not every question that deserves an answer."
Maxim 581

Even a fool who keeps silent is considered wise; when he closes his lips, he is deemed intelligent.
Proverbs 17:28

Before we speak, we should consider:

- How will my words impact others?
- Am I sowing peace, kindness, and love?
- Do I have anything worthwhile to contribute?

"We are masters of the unsaid words, but slaves of those we let slip out."
Winston Churchill

REFLECTION

MAKE A LIST OF SOME REALLY IMPRESSIVE THINGS
YOU HAVE SEEN GOD DO IN YOUR LIFE.
HOW WILL YOU SHARE THEM WITH OTHERS?

November 30
Divine Abundance

And he said to them,"Take heed, and beware of all covetousness;
for man's life does not consist in the abundance of his possessions."
Luke 12:15

There was a wealthy man who wanted his son to appreciate how blessed he was to be rich. He took his son to an impoverished land where he could see how the very poor people lived. Upon leaving, he asked, "Son, what have you learned?"

The son replied, "We have one dog, they have four. We have a swimming pool, they have a creek that doesn't end. We have a small piece of land to live on, they have fields that go beyond sight. We have locks on our doors and an alarm system, they have friends to protect them. Thanks, Dad, I did not realize how poor we were."

True riches are found in good health, freedom from fear, harmonious relationships, wisdom, realizing our God-given purpose, and a genuine appreciation of God's creation. There is nothing sinful about having earthly success, but not at the expense of spiritual growth. Cultivating appreciation for true riches generates spiritual growth.

With divine abundance, the only limit is in our capacity to believe and receive.

On the glorious splendor of Thy majesty,
and on Thy wondrous works, I will meditate.
Psalm 145:5

Thou openest Thy hand, Thou satisfiest the desire of every living thing.
Psalm 145:16

REFLECTION

HOW DO YOU FIND REAL CONTENTMENT?

December 1

Avoiding Sin Is Only Part of the Process

"Submit yourselves therefore to God.
Resist the devil and he will flee from you.
James 4:7

We work really hard to avoid sin. It is difficult to avoid sin. Getting rid of a sinful behavior or removing ourselves from temptations is only half the battle.

When we trust our own strength to resist temptation, we are probably going to fall short at some point. It is only when we replace that resistance with love of God and His service that we begin to get it right.

Our sinfulness is often the result of seeking love, respect, or security in our lives through some worldly resource. The power of sin increases as we pursue satisfaction of these needs. The longer we pursue these needs, the harder it is to resist sin and break the habits we have developed in the process.

Submission to God rescues us from the grip of sin. God is always there, and God knows our sin and the power it has over us. God loves and accepts us anyway, just the way we are. The more we allow Him to come into our lives and fill the void that sin creates, the more fulfilled we are.

Draw near to God and he will draw near to you. Cleanse your hands,
you sinners, and purify your hearts, you men of double mind.
James 4:8

REFLECTION

RIGHT NOW, TODAY, WHERE DO YOU NEED TO "DO WORK"
IN YOUR LIFE? RIGHT NOW, TODAY, WHERE DO YOU NEED
TO DEMONSTRATE YOUR SUBMISSION?

December 2

Now Is the Acceptable Time

Working together with him, then, we entreat you not to accept the grace of God in vain. For he says, "At the acceptable time I have listened to you and helped you on the day of salvation."
2 Corinthians 6:1-2

Now is the acceptable time. Now is the day of salvation. Now is the time to demonstrate our love for God and all that He has done for us.

Wherever you are in your walk with God, now is the time to share your faith with others. Now is the time to trust, obey, and proceed with the life God has called you to live.

You know what is right. You know what is good. You know what is true. Let your life reflect your love of God and your love for others—total, unconditional, and complete love.

We are treated as impostors, and yet are true; as unknown, and yet well known; as dying, and behold we live; as punished, and yet not killed; as sorrowful, yet always rejoicing; as poor, yet making many rich; as having nothing, and yet possessing everything.
2 Corinthians 6:8-10

REFLECTION

HOW COULD YOU ENCOURAGE A FRIEND,
FAMILY MEMBER, OR CO-WORKER TODAY?

December 3
Why Are You Afraid?

"Why are you afraid? Have you no faith?"
Mark 4:40

The storm raged, waves beat into the boat and the boat was being swamped. Jesus was asleep in the stern, and His disciples were in panic. They woke Him and expressed their concern.

Jesus calmed the storm and asked them why they were afraid. In the simple context, this is another miracle performed by Jesus in the presence of His disciples.

However, the greater context was that they were afraid. The Bible tells us not to fear. That message is delivered scores of times in the words "fear not," and the message is communicated many more times with different wording.

The truly faithful follower has no fear of anything this world can deliver.

...fear not, for I am with you, be not dismayed, for I am your God;
I will strengthen you, I will help you,
I will uphold you with my victorious right hand.
Isaiah 41:10

REFLECTION

WHAT ARE YOU AFRAID OF? HOW DO YOU OVERCOME FEAR?

December 4

God Is Watching

For the eyes of the Lord run to and fro throughout the whole earth, to show his might in behalf of those whose heart is blameless toward him.
2 Chronicles 16:9

God is watching over us. He is not watching to see us fail or sin but to provide fatherly protection and love. He is not a passively involved parent unless we want it that way.

God knows we are tempted. He also knows that we will fall into sin because we are only human. That is why He entered our lives and became flesh in order to make the blood sacrifice necessary to give atonement for and forgive the sins of everyone.

No temptation has overtaken you that is not common to man. God is faithful, and he will not let you be tempted beyond your strength, but with the temptation will also provide the way of escape, that you may be able to endure it.
1 Corinthians 10:13

REFLECTION

WHEN YOU PRAY, HOW DO YOU FEEL ABOUT GOD?

December 5

The Eye of the Needle

*"It is easier for a camel to go through the eye of a needle
than for a rich man to enter the kingdom of God."*
Mark 10:25

A wall for defense surrounded most important cities in those days. The wall had a large gate which remained open during the day but was closed at night. There was usually a smaller gate set in the big door or close by called "the eye of a needle." This gate could be opened to allow entry to those who arrived after sunset. In order to bring a camel through the small door, everything had to be removed from its back so it could enter. The camel was not able to enter the gate with its burden.

Those "possessions" which keep us from entering the kingdom of God may come in many forms.

The material possessions seem evident—money, property, financial wellbeing. There is also passion for physical pleasures, lust, greed, control of others, and personal ambitions.

Having possessions is not a bad thing. Most of the instructions from Jesus contain a message of stewardship in how to manage earthly possessions. Many of our possessions are a result of a fruitful existence, blessings God has given us for obedient, productive living. However, it is dependence on material possessions and the passions raised by the need for possessions and power that keep us from entering the kingdom of God, which is available here, now, right where we are.

REFLECTION

WHAT EXPENSE, ACTIVITY, OR CONCERN COULD YOU
ELIMINATE TODAY THAT WOULD SIMPLIFY YOUR LIFE?

December 6

Tomorrow

I can do all things in him who strengthens me.
Philippians 4:13

A woman diagnosed with stage 4, severe cancer, sold her home and many of her possessions. She moved into a retirement community, apprehensive about making new friends and facing the major changes in her daily routine. She summoned the courage to be outgoing and friendly to everyone she met. The people she met responded in similar fashion with friendly, happy, and encouraging greetings and conversation. As she forgot about herself and made a deliberate effort to learn about them, she decided to write a book as she had always wanted to do but "never had the time." She decided the book would be about these new friends, their stories, and the impact her friends had on the world.

It is never too late to do those things you "never had the time to do." Right now, today, you are more experienced than you have ever been. You are wiser than ever before. You have a different perspective on everything than you have ever had. Be open to God's direction toward unexpected paths for you. Take on a new challenge with courage and maybe even joy!

REFLECTION

WHAT POSITIVE CHANGES HAVE YOU MADE IN YOUR LIFE THIS YEAR?

December 7

Power, Love, and Self-Control

...I remind you to rekindle the gift of God that is within you ...
2 Timothy 1:6

Paul wrote two letters to Timothy. These letters were intended to encourage Timothy as he confronted the challenges in Ephesus.

As Paul urges Timothy to endure hardship and "rekindle the gift of God," Paul faces challenges of his own. His closing words in 2 Timothy 4:6-8 indicate that he is facing his own martyrdom with courage, conviction, and love of God.

Following Christ, leading the life God would have you lead, is not always an easy path. Many Christians are fortunate to enjoy the freedom to worship God, but many others face the prospect of punishment or even death for claiming the Christian faith. For those of us who enjoy the freedom to worship, there may be everyday hardships that create roadblocks for us...the desire for worldly goods, social peer pressure, shaming, fear of being "different," and the like confront us daily. The Lord knows our circumstances. Paul would tell us to rekindle the gifts we have from God, be strong, and keep the faith!

...for God did not give us a spirit of timidity
but a spirit of power and love and self-control.
Timothy 1:7

REFLECTION

HOW DOES PAUL'S VIEW OF SERVICE, LIFE, DEATH,
DEVOTION, AND DUTY APPLY IN YOUR LIFE?

December 8

Patient Endurance

"Because you have kept my word of patient endurance,
I will keep you from the hour of trial which is coming
on the whole world..."
Revelation 3:10

Faith is confidence, a robust, vigorous confidence based on the fact that God is love. The truly faithful view the circumstances of this world with "patient endurance" by accepting God's love. They accept all conditions as His—His timing, His purpose, and His plan.

When we do this, our lives can become a beautiful romance, full of wonderful opportunities to see His glory in all things all the time.

Now faith is the assurance of things hoped for,
the conviction of things not seen.
Hebrews 11:1

REFLECTION

IN WHAT SITUATIONS TODAY ARE YOU LOOKING
FOR GOD TO EXPRESS HIS PRESENCE?

December 9

Watch Your Tongue

So the tongue is a little member and boasts of great things.
How great a forest is set ablaze by a small fire!
James 3:5-6

Our words are far more powerful than we think. Words can have a ripple effect beyond the immediate circumstances that generate them. People remember words not as they may have been intended but as they were received.

Build a verbal firewall that limits your words to words of praise, thanksgiving, and good intentions. Speak as if you are accountable to God, because you are.

"...for by your words you will be justified, and
by your words you will be condemned."
Matthew 12:37

REFLECTION

WHAT WISDOM DO YOU SEEK FROM GOD?
HOW DO YOU THINK GOD IS ANSWERING YOU?

December 10

Iron Sharpens Iron

Iron sharpens iron, and one man sharpens another.
Proverbs 28:17

We all have times of weakness, events, and circumstances that challenge our moral fiber.

It is in times like these that having strong relationships with people of faith will enable us to grow through the hard times.

It is also important to share good news with people we are close to. Celebration is not nearly as much fun when we are alone as when we are able to engage with people who share our values and appreciate our reasons to celebrate. They sharpen us and we sharpen them on our faith journeys.

Show yourself in all respects a model of good deeds,
and in your teaching show integrity, gravity...
Titus 2:7

REFLECTION

WHO DO YOU KNOW WHO NEEDS SPIRITUAL ENCOURAGEMENT?

HOW CAN YOU PROVIDE THAT FOR THEM?

December 11

He Teaches Us

...for he was teaching his disciples...
Mark 9:31

Following the teachings of Jesus will help us become more Christ-like. With discipline, reverence, and faith, we learn, and we can become a new person.

God provides each of us with talents and abilities to become... to become a vital component to His plan...to become what He wants us to be.

He gives us both adversity and prosperity to define and refine those talents and abilities and to develop skills that will enable us to accomplish His purpose.

And God said to him (Solomon), "Because you have asked this, and have not asked for yourself long life or riches or the life of your enemies but have asked for yourself understanding to discern what is right, behold, I now do according to your word. Behold, I give you a wise and discerning mind...I give you also what you have not asked, both riches and honor...and if you will walk in my ways, keeping my statutes and my commandments...then I will lengthen your days.
1 Kings 3:11-13

REFLECTION

HOW WILL YOUR CURRENT CIRCUMSTANCES HELP YOU
GROW THIS DAY IN JOY, PEACE, AND HAPPINESS?

December 12

Confession

*If we confess our sins, he is faithful and just, and will
forgive our sins and cleanse us from all unrighteousness.*
1 John 1:9

As believers, our sins are forgiven, and they do not break our relationship with God, but they do interfere with our personal fellowship with Him. We can restore that fellowship with confession.

Face facts, do not try to explain them away. We must sincerely repent, ask for forgiveness, and then release what has happened. It is our choice to confess and when we do, God's forgiveness is total; a precious gift that we cannot appreciate enough.

And because God has forgiven us, we must focus on what we are going to make happen in our lives and in our relationship with God from the lessons learned.

*Let us hold fast the confession of our hope without wavering,
for he who promised is faithful.*
Hebrews 10:23

REFLECTION

WHEN AND HOW HAVE YOU FELT GOD'S FATHERLY FORGIVENESS
AND ACCEPTANCE IN SPITE OF YOUR DISOBEDIENCE?

December 13

Frailty

For the sake of Christ, then, I am content with weaknesses,
insults, hardships, persecutions, and calamities;
for when I am weak, then I am strong.
2 Corinthians 12:10

Paul suffered from a debilitating ailment. We do not know exactly what this ailment was, but he refers to it several times in his letters. This weakness of Paul's physical body gave him a greater appreciation for God's grace in his life.

Physical weakness is a human condition that all of us will ultimately suffer. It is spiritual strength that makes us truly strong. Spiritual strength enables us to face difficulties and overcome human problems. Through spiritual strength we see the beauty in this world and the hope of the world to come.

Likewise, the Spirit helps us in our weakness;
for we do not know how to pray as we ought, but the Spirit himself
intercedes for us with sighs too deep for words.
Romans 8:26

REFLECTION

WHAT SITUATIONS OR PEOPLE
COULD YOU BLESS RATHER THAN BLAME?

December 14

Personal Peace

Her ways are ways of pleasantness, and all her paths are peace.
Proverbs 3:17

"Peace I leave with you, my peace I give unto you."
John 14:27

Thou dost keep him in perfect peace,
whose mind is stayed on thee, because he trusts in thee.
Isaiah 26:3

Personal peace is a state of mind that places God and God's will clearly in control. When our mind is controlled by the matters of this world, when we are not placing God first in our lives, the results are not what God wants for us. This does not mean we are to ignore the matters of this world. They are here to serve a purpose in our lives and in the lives of others. However, these matters take on a whole new perspective when we put God first and view them in His light.

To maintain a balanced, vigorous mental life, we have to overcome external forces using an internal vitality that is provided by the Spirit. Spiritual growth develops internal peace and reflects external strength.

For the kingdom of God is not food and drink but righteousness
and peace and joy in the Holy Spirit.
Romans 14:17

Let us then pursue what makes for peace and for mutual upbuilding...
Romans 14:19

REFLECTION

WHAT LESSONS ABOUT LOVE HAS GOD TAUGHT YOU RECENTLY?

December 15

Marital Responsibility

Be subject to one another out of reverence for Christ. Wives,
be subject to your husbands, as to the Lord. ...
Husbands, love your wives, as Christ loved the church
and gave himself up for her...
Ephesians 5:21-22, 25

How often we see marriages that include 1 Corinthians 13:4-7. "Love is patient and kind; love is not jealous or boastful; it is not arrogant or rude. Love does not insist on its own way; it is not irritable or resentful; it does not rejoice at wrong but rejoices in the right. Love bears all things, believes all things, hopes all things, endures all things. Love never ends..."

And then things change. Marriages do not fail, people do. When couples are "subject to one another out of reverence for Christ" things are very different. Their marriages are happier and often last longer. The true secret of success in marriage, or in any significant relationship, is being subject to one another out of reverence for Christ.

REFLECTION

WHAT WAYS CAN YOU STRENGTHEN YOUR MARRIAGE
OR A SIGNIFICANT RELATIONSHIP IN YOUR LIFE?"

December 16

Avoid Falling

*In the last time there will be scoffers, following their own
ungodly passions. It is these who set up divisions,
worldly people, devoid of the Spirit.*
Jude 1:18

Jude sent his short letter to warn about false teachers who were
penetrating the church. These people were immoral and covetous, loud mouthed boasters, and malcontents. Their purpose was
to disrupt, derail, and destroy the church. He urges his readers to
"contend for the faith" and build themselves up on their faith.

We do not know who the author was, but some scholars believe he was one of the brothers of Jesus. Jude wraps up his message
with a beautiful and concise message of praise. In this verse, he
describes not only salvation from sin, but salvation into God's
glory with rejoicing, welcoming us into the Light which is God's
presence.

*Now to him who is able to keep you from falling and to present you
without blemish before the presence of his glory with rejoicing, to the
only God, our Savior through Jesus Christ our Lord, be glory, majesty,
dominion, and authority, before all time and now and for ever.
Amen.*
Jude 1:24

REFLECTION

HOW HAS GOD PLACED YOU IN THE LIVES OF OTHERS
AS A PERSON OF INFLUENCE?

December 17

God and Mammon

"No one can serve two masters; for either he will hate the one and love the other, or he will be devoted to the one and despise the other. You cannot serve God and mammon."
Matthew 6:24

Mammon is a Semitic word meaning money or riches. We cannot serve God and serve money or riches at the same time. The key concept here is "serve." Serve in this case means to be a servant to, wait on, dance attendance to. We have two choices. One offers limitation, the other offers eternal rewards.

Money and riches are finite, limited to this world, and the rewards for serving them are limited. God wants to provide abundance in our lives. The abundance that rewards service to God has no limits, no boundaries, and is ever expanding and eternal.

"But seek first his kingdom and his righteousness, and all these things shall be yours as well."
Matthew 6:33

REFLECTION

HOW HAS YOUR LIFE CHANGED
AS A RESULT OF YOUR RELATIONSHIP WITH GOD?

December 18

Who We Serve

As each has received a gift, employ it for one another,
as good stewards of God's varied grace...
1 Peter 4:10

Whatever gifts we possess, we are to use them in service to benefit others. How do we do this?

Pray for direction. There are many who need the gifts we have. Not all of them are in homeless shelters or soup kitchens. We may need to serve a co-worker, a neighbor, or even a member of our church.

Start with Jesus and His example. Then, look around. Offer what you have to others. This may be your talent for organization, your passion for beauty, or even your ability to sit and listen. Also, pray for discernment. There are many who would take advantage of you. If that happens, it is their loss, not yours. However, while you were serving them, someone else was missing the gifts you had to offer.

...whoever renders service, as one who renders it by the strength
which God supplies; in order that in everything God
may be glorified through Jesus Christ. To him belong glory
and dominion for ever and ever.
1 Peter 4:11

REFLECTION

WHO BROUGHT YOU TO CHRIST? HOW? WHEN? WHERE?

December 19

The Vine and Us

*Abide in me, and I in you. As the branch cannot bear fruit by itself,
unless it abides in the vine, neither can you, unless you abide in me.*
John 15:4

*These things I have spoken to you, that my joy may be in you,
and that your joy may be full.*
John 15:11

We, as followers, are told to bear fruit. The fruit is often expressed in our praise and joy as a result of our passion for Jesus and the faith we have.

In order to produce the right fruit, we must stay attached to the Vine. Unfortunately, in our enthusiasm, we may attempt to be our own vine.

Looking for joy and praising matters of this world will ultimately lead to stress and anxiety. We cannot produce the joy on our own. Our pleasure, our passion, and our fruit must come from our relationship with God.

*Thou dost show me the path of life; in thy presence
there is fullness of joy,
in thy right hand are pleasures for evermore.*
Psalm 16:11

REFLECTION

WHERE HAS GOD CALLED THAT YOU DID NOT GO?

December 20

Pray Now

...now is the day of salvation.
1 Corinthians 6:2

There are many ways to guide your prayers. One is described by the acronym ACTS: Adoration, Confession, Thanksgiving, and Supplication.

A: Speak words of **A**doration to Almighty God. Be fulsome. Use imagery. Rejoice in the Lord!

C: **C**onfess your shortcoming—acts of commission and acts omission. Repent sincerely. Pray over the things that caused you to fall short, to sin. Be fully contrite and ask for forgiveness.

T: Be **T**hankful. There are always blessings to be found. Yes, sometimes it takes a little more searching to fill out your blessing list, but blessings are there. Let your heart fill with gratitude for God's goodness and His mercy.

S: And offer up your **S**upplications. Tell God about your needs. Remember, He already knows your heart and your mind. Talk to Him about your fears, your challenges, your pain. Ask for wisdom and courage when you need it. Seek advice and keep yourself open to receive answers or direction. Pray for comfort and assurance when you are feeling bereft and alone. Be truly in His presence while you commune with Him. Ask in the spirit of God's love and His will for His children.

Take this moment to pray, elevate your thoughts to the spiritual realm, and spend some time with your heavenly Father.

...as servants of God we commend ourselves in every way: through great endurance, in afflictions, hardships, calamities, beatings, imprisonments, tumults, labors, watching, hunger...
II Corinthians 6:4-5

REFLECTION

WHAT IS YOUR UNDERSTANDING OF ACCEPTING JESUS IN YOUR LIFE?

December 21

Your Heart's Desire

Take delight in the Lord, and he will give you
the desires of your heart.
Psalm 37:4

The universe is a unified harmony, a divine plan. What you call your heart's desire, that most secret wish that lies at the very bottom of your heart, is what you are called to do for God in His divine plan. God knows your every thought and desire. He planted the good seed of a true heart's desire. Revel in the gift of your life's passion. Use it to God's glory. Be full of thanksgiving.

"You did not choose me, but I chose you and appointed you that you
should go and bear fruit and that your fruit should abide;
so that whatever you ask the Father in my name,
he may give it to you."
John 15:16

REFLECTION

WHAT DO YOU HONESTLY WANT TO DISCUSS WITH GOD TODAY?

WHAT STOPS YOU?

December 22

Be Still and Know

Be still, and know that I am God.
Psalm 46:10

We can look at wonderful images of the Grand Canyon and see gorgeous colors and shapes in two dimensions but nothing can replace the experience of being in the midst the real grandeur.

Reading and studying about God give us knowledge to prepare us for a deeper, more intimate or personal experience in the presence of God. We may experience God's presence in any number of ways, but we must "be still and know"…be open, attuned, attentive in heart and spirit to receive the experience.

"…and you shall love the Lord your God with all your heart,
and with all your soul, and with all your mind,
and with all your strength."
Mark 12:30

REFLECTION

HOW DO YOU RESPOND TO THOSE SITUATIONS
THAT REQUIRE PATIENCE AND WAITING?

December 23

Watch

And he came to the disciples and found them sleeping;
and he said to Peter, "So, could you not watch with me one hour?"
Matthew 26:40

There is a world of difference between watching for Jesus and watching with Jesus. In this passage, Jesus is talking to Peter, probably His closest disciple, who had gone to sleep while Jesus prayed at Gethsemane. As with many of His comments, the disciples would not understand until after the resurrection.

It is like this with us, too. Watching "with" Jesus sheds an entirely different light on the world around us. People, all people, are to be loved, not judged. Things are just that, things. Possessions are not ours, everything belongs to God, and we are entrusted with some of it to be stewards, protecting, preserving, and returning them.

Watch and pray that you may not enter into temptation;
the spirit indeed is willing, but the flesh is weak.
Matthew 26:41

REFLECTION

WHAT ARE YOU WATCHING FOR?
HOW DO YOU THINK IT WILL BE REVEALED?

December 24

Be Holy

"You shall be holy, for I am holy…"
1 Peter 1:16

Continually restate to yourself what the purpose of your life is. Our destiny is not happiness, but holiness…unsullied walking, talking, and thinking. Holiness is what God gives us and we manifest for others.

He loves us. Forgiveness and total acceptance of us just the way we are are the result of love. Often our most difficult task is to forgive ourselves as He has forgiven us and proceed with being productive in His purpose.

Fill your heart with love. Think about, feel, and express love in all places and in doing all things. When you think, feel, and express love in all circumstances, love will show the solution to any problem and the way to overcome any difficulty.

REFLECTION

WHAT DO YOU THINK IS THE MAIN PURPOSE OF YOUR LIFE?

December 25
A Christmas Message

*In the beginning was the Word, and the Word was with God, and the
Word was God. He was in the beginning with God; all things were
made through him, and without him was not anything made that
was made. In him was life, and the life was the light of men.
The light shines in the darkness, and the darkness has not overcome it.*
John 1:1-5

*And the Word became flesh and dwelt among us,
full of grace and truth; we have beheld his glory,
glory as of the only Son from the Father.*
John 1:14

God's entry into our world was in order to direct us, bless us, and save us from the ultimate consequences of our sinful nature.

*"The Son of God became a man to enable men
to become the sons of God."*
C.S. Lewis

The symbolic sequence reflects the perfection of God's plan.

Due to circumstances beyond their control, Mary and Joseph could not find a place to stay. An innkeeper who had no rooms in his inn offered his stable with a manger to them.

Normally, food for sheep is placed in a manger. Sheep are often used metaphorically to give us lessons in following, trusting, and accepting the guidance of the shepherd.

Christmas is the Spirit of God. Consider the wonder and awe of this day and this season and make it the centerpiece of your

Holiday Season and throughout the coming year.

The true message of Christmas is hope. God has dominion over all things. God wants what is best for the people He loves so dearly, and He will provide what is best for them if they will allow it.

REFLECTION

HOW WILL YOU SHARE YOUR JOY THIS CHRISTMAS SEASON?

December 26

Just Ask

But ask the beasts, and they will teach you; the birds of the air, and they will tell you; or the plants of the earth, and they will teach you; and the fish of the sea will declare to you. Who among all these does not know that the hand of the Lord has done this? In his hand is the life of every living thing and the breath of all mankind.
Job 12:7-10

What we call nature is a very small part of God's universe. We only begin to understand His nature when we study and appreciate these things.

There are millions of things happening all the time that we cannot see or understand. Consider the depths of the sea and the sustained balance of life there. Then consider the natural impact of sun, stars, and the composition of what we know as the heavens.

And yet, He still has all of the time we want to talk with Him.

With God are wisdom and might;
he has counsel and understanding.
Job 12:13

REFLECTION

GOD MAKES TIME FOR YOU. HOW ARE YOU MAKING TIME FOR GOD?

December 27

From Victory, Not for Victory

*...no weapon that is fashioned against you shall prosper, and you shall
confute every tongue that rises against you in judgment.
This is the heritage of the servants of the LORD
and their vindication from me, says the LORD.*
Isaiah 54:17

Time after time in Old Testament accounts of God's people
against formidable enemies, His people win, often against in-
credible odds.

Our spiritual life, while blessed, is one of constant battle. It's a
battle against the forces of evil, the temptations of this world, and
the emotional turmoil of adverse circumstances. Many times, the
stress of facing any challenge is that we don't know how it's going
to end. That is not the case with our spiritual battle.

The big difference in this battle is that we are fighting from a
victory that has already been won by Jesus, not for a victory which
is uncertain.

*...for not by their own sword did they win the land, nor did their
own arm give them victory; but thy right hand, and thy arm,
and the light of thy countenance; for thou didst delight in them.*
Psalm 44:3

REFLECTION

WHAT BATTLES WILL YOU FACE DURING THE COMING YEAR?
HOW DO YOU WANT GOD TO PARTICIPATE?

December 28

Never Water Down the Word of God

...the righteous are bold as a lion...
Proverbs 28:1

Never water down the word of God. Tell it in its undiluted fullness.

God has placed you where your service will be most effective. Read, study, meditate, and pray for wisdom and direction. Then, do not hesitate to tell it like it is. There are those who need to hear your testimony. There are those whose lives will be changed by your witness. Do not deny them by being shy about your faith.

Remember who you are—a sinner saved by grace. Everyone you meet is also a sinner, and anyone can be saved by grace.

...but one thing I do, forgetting what lies behind and straining for what lies ahead. I press on toward the goal for the prize of the upward call of God in Christ Jesus.
Philippians 12:13

REFLECTION

HOW HAS YOUR FAITH GROWN OR DIMINISHED THIS YEAR?
WHY IS THIS SO?

December 29

The Company We Keep

He who walks with wise men becomes wise,
but the companion of fools will suffer harm.
Proverbs 13:20

Peer pressure has a lot of influence on our behavior. The company we keep provides that peer pressure. If we remain in the company of faithful people, there is still temptation, but it is far easier to handle than if our peer group is cheering us on to unacceptable actions.

There is more than enough unacceptable pressure on people today with social, print, and television media. There is also the temptation to enter into negative relationships, especially out of sympathy.

It just makes good sense to spend most of our time walking, talking, and working with wise and encouraging people who help us grow closer to Christ.

REFLECTION

HOW DOES GOD'S WORD
INFLUENCE THE WAY YOU APPROACH DAILY LIFE?

December 30

That I May Know Him

Commit your actions to the Lord, and your plans will be established.
Proverbs 16:3

Those who seek spiritual fulfillment look for God's presence in every circumstance. Wherever they are placed, they know that it is not by chance, but that they are placed there by God for His purpose.

> *"But seek ye first his kingdom and his righteousness,*
> *and all these things shall be yours as well."*
> **Matthew 6:33**

Our personal contributions may seem insignificant in worldly terms. However, when we are genuinely seeking to see, feel, and express God's presence in everything we encounter, we may not see the good we are doing. In fact, the work we do may not bear fruit for months, years, or even generations. The important thing is that we do what we do knowing that God is at work in and through our lives.

> *And the LORD will make himself known ...*
> **Isaiah 19:21**

> *...make every effort to add to your faith goodness; and to goodness,*
> *knowledge; and to knowledge, self-control; and to self-control,*
> *perseverance; and to perseverance, godliness; and to godliness,*
> *brotherly kindness, and to brotherly kindness, love...*
> **2 Peter 1:5-7**

REFLECTION

REFLECTING OVER THE PAST YEAR, WHAT ACTIONS DID YOU
TAKE THAT SEEMED INSIGNIFICANT BUT RESULTED IN
UNANTICIPATED LEARNING OR REWARDS?

December 31

Think, Plan, Pray

The plans of the diligent lead surely to abundance,
but everyone who is hasty comes only to want.
Proverbs 21:5

Think, plan, pray. Do this constantly, consistently, faithfully. Enter the new year with deliberate steps toward positive goals, knowing that you are loved, encouraged, and supported by God.

Listen to God. Listen to your own inner voice. Seek ambitious and abundant accomplishments.

Never sell yourself short. Never give up. Never forget that you are the cherished child of God. God's plans and desires for you far exceed anything you can desire or pray for.

Think big. If that doesn't work, think bigger!

Never look back, God is always on the road ahead.

REFLECTION

WHAT IS GOD PUTTING ON YOUR HEART
TO DO THIS COMING YEAR?

Made in the USA
Columbia, SC
12 April 2022

58567299R10213